Art Under the Microscope

Discovering the Scientific World with Artistic Eyes

GIA CLARKE
LUCY SHI

ART UNDER THE MICROSCOPE
Discovering the Scientific World with Artistic Eyes
by Gia Clarke and Lucy Ruoxi Shi
1. JNF051110–JUVENILE NONFICTION / Science & Nature / Experiments & Projects
2. JNF051050–JUVENILE NONFICTION / Science & Nature / Biology
3. JNF051000–JUVENILE NONFICTION / Science & Nature / General

ISBN: 979-8-88636-003-5 (paperback)
ISBN: 979-8-88636-004-2 (ebook)

Cover and interior photos by the authors

Printed in the United States of America

Authority Publishing
11230 Gold Express Dr. #310-413
Gold River, CA 95670
800-877-1097
www.AuthorityPublishing.com

I have dedicated my career to educating elementary aged students for decades, I am thrilled to see a science book written for young children by young children. This wonderfully illustrated book bridges science and art, drawing the attention of children of all ages. Readers will be both fascinated by the science and stimulated by the authors' creativity and artistry. I am proud of the accomplishments of these young children, and I hope it will inspire more children to explore the beauty and wonder of the natural world through scientific inquiry and keep them wondering about the world around them.

Stay curious!

Kathy Flores
Principal, Westwood Charter Elementary

The way children view and approach the world is truly fascinating. Their boundless imaginations and effortless curiosity make them natural scientists. These attributes are on full display in this wonderful work that creatively merges scientific inquiry with artistic expression.

In *Art Under the Microscope*, we have the rare privilege to observe the tiny structures that make up common plants through the gaze of young budding scientists. It is a tour de force through this microscopic world. The enthusiasm and depth of understanding that they share with us is truly special. It is something that we all should strive to spark in our children in cultivating interest in science, technology, engineering, arts, and mathematics education. I hope that this book inspires our future innovative scientists, engineers, and healthcare providers to take a look for themselves under the microscope. I'm excited to see what they see!

Steven Jonas, MD, PhD
UCLA Health Pediatrician / Scientist

Acknowledgments

Our team here had the wonderful pleasure of getting help and support from so many people we'd like to thank:

Dr. Zhu, who is a professor and pathologist, for giving us the time and permission to use the microscope in her office, and for also helping us form the idea of a botanical atlas by showing what a human pathology atlas looks like.

Additionally, we give lots of thanks to **Ryan Zhang**, who taught all of us how to prepare the slides, and the fundamentals of the microscope.

Lots of thanks also go to the wonderful team, including **Alex Wu**, who is excellent at cross-sectioning the plants, **Patrick Tseng**, **Tiffany Zhang**, and **Ellen Sun** for their advice and suggestions.

Last but not least, we thank the reader for taking the time to read and enjoy this book!

Thank you!

Preface

It all started with two curious minds and a meeting.

We came upon an odd image and discovered that it was a lily flower underneath a microscope. We were curious and surprised when we noticed that it looked like a famous cartoon. We began observing even more closely and noticed several other small details that reminded us of other small drawings around the image. We started drawing on the image ourselves, and soon, an idea formed between us. We started talking and thought, *why don't we make our own microscopic images and then create drawings from them?*

And so it began.

We are Gia and Lucy.

We began this project by scouring our kitchens and gardens for plants that could be observed under the microscope. We sought the help of Professor Zhu, a pathologist at UCLA and who gave us the time and permission to use her office to explore our samples under the lens of the key to this project: **the microscope.**

With the help of Ryan Zhang, a UCLA Research Assistant and Professor Zhu's colleague, we learned the proper way to prepare slides, and how to adjust the magnification. We learned everything from soaking in Ethanol, to dying in ink, to rinsing in water. After a while, we had a large collection of microscopic samples. The magnification levels were 4x, 10x, 20x, and 40x. When multiplied with the lens magnification levels (as is done), they became 40x, 100x, 200x, and 400x. Surprised by the amazing images under the microscope, we had the idea of making a botanical atlas featuring the plants that were readily available in our daily life. With the help of a team cutting plants, preparing slides, and taking pictures using a microscope, we were able to write about and image a wide variety of plants.

In this book, each image taken by the microscope will be accompanied by an illustration incorporating the original image. Each picture will also have a short text describing the parts of the plant imaged. This botanical atlas was envisioned to show how beautiful the botanical specimens look under a microscope by comparing each scientific picture and caption with its artistic counterpart. The comparison bridges the gap between science and art for you to read and learn.

We hope you enjoy!

About Us

Gia Clarke

Gia is a fifth grader who has an inclination for many things. One of her favorite hobbies is art, and her favorite types of art are watercolor and sketching. Gia also loves to design: jewelry, fashion, interiors, and more! In her spare time, she enjoys ballet, volleyball, swimming, piano, reading, baking...and the list goes on!

Lucy Ruoxi Shi

Lucy is a sixth grader and an avid artist who enjoys playing volleyball, singing songs from Disney movies to entertain people, and reading everything she can (though she generally prefers books) in her spare time. Lucy loves her iPad, using it to animate and draw things, including many of the drawings in this book.

How We Did It

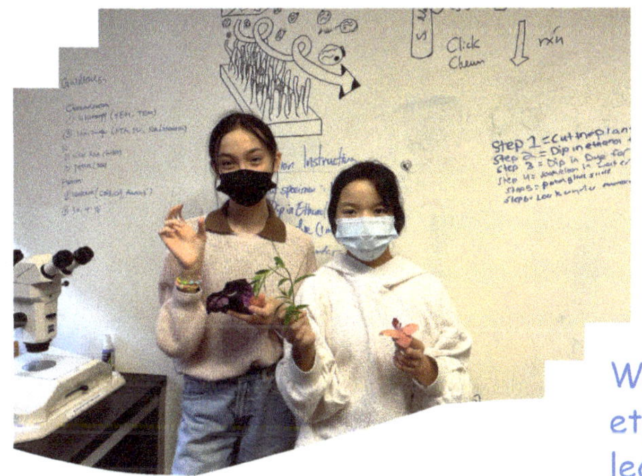

We hand-selected a variety of fresh greens collected from various local sources around us.

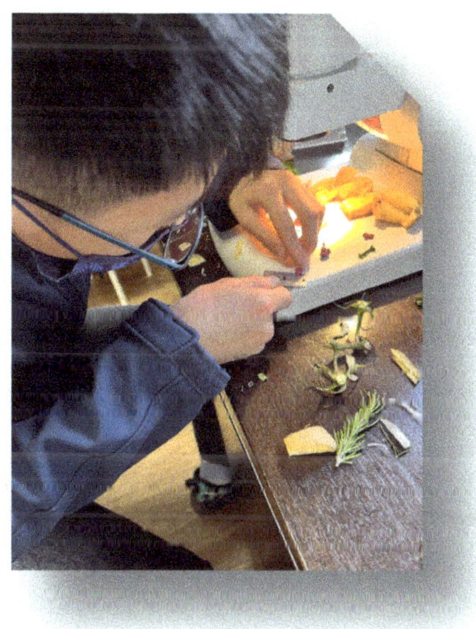

To start, we cut our specimens into thin, small pieces. The typical ways of preparing a plant include cross-sectioning and longitudinal sectioning. To avoid black splotches here and there on the samples, we also made sure that the plants we were examining were clean.

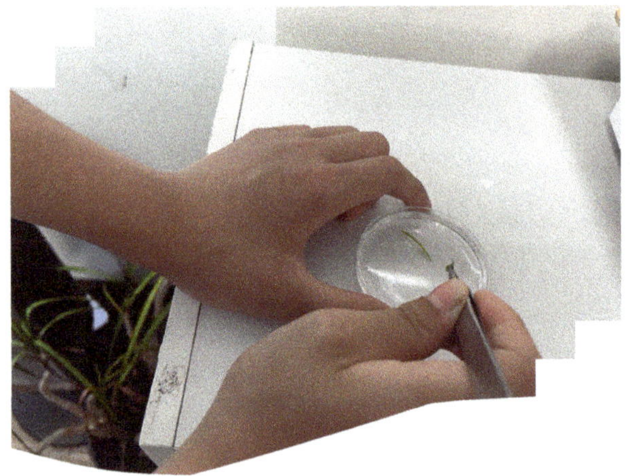

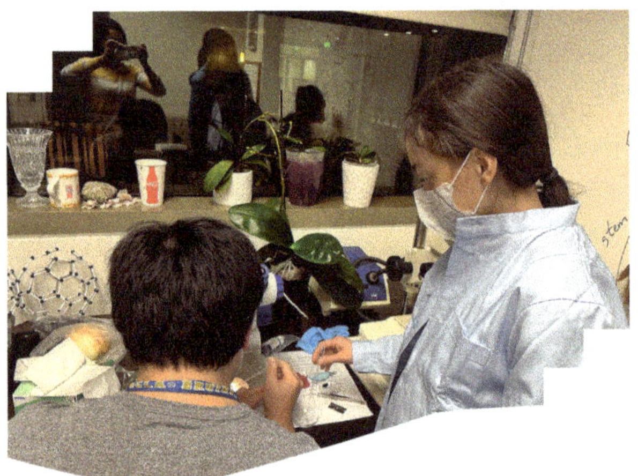

We then picked them up with tweezers, dipping them into the first bowl: Ethanol. We use tweezers to make sure we didn't lose the sample in one of the solutions, and to pick it up when we were done with it.

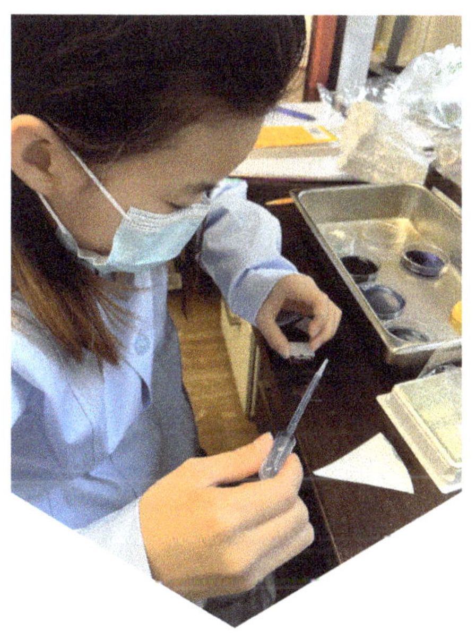

Ethanol was used to dehydrate the specimen, and when we were done, we put it in the dye. For our samples, we mainly used 1% toluidine blue, soaking it for about a minute (we did overstain a few samples and learned, for future reference, to only soak for one minute so that the sample doesn't become too dehydrated and soak up too much ink, which makes it impossible to see the cells as clearly).

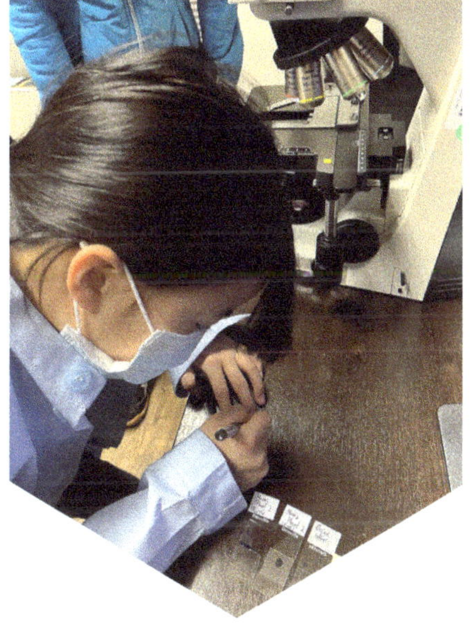

When the dye staining was over, we rinsed it in water (this picks up excess ink). Then, we placed it on a glass slide, putting a drop of water on it so the cover slide would stick. Finally, we placed the cover slide carefully over it to secure it.

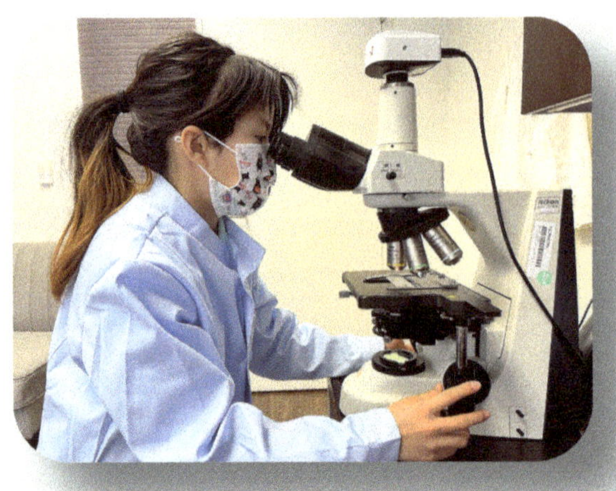

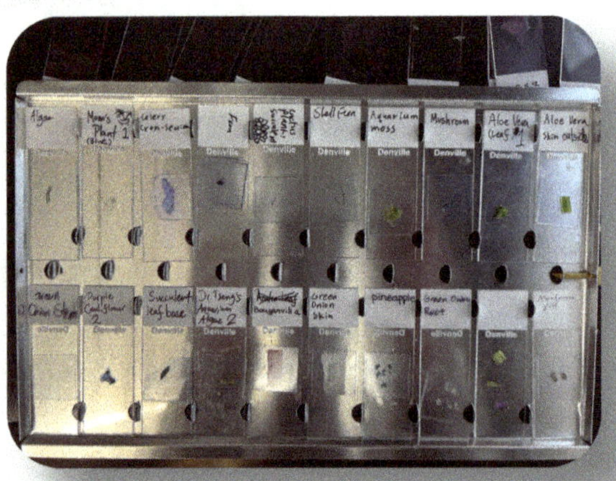

We labeled each slide for record. To observe the specimen properly, we placed it underneath the microscope, securing it with the slide clip. There were so many things to see! We were able to adjust the knobs from 4x to 10x to 20x to 40x, offering different levels of magnification.

We are really glad to bring you along for the journey. So without further ado, let's get into it!

Table of Contents

Part B: Flowers and Leaves

Part A

Fruits and Vegetables

Avocado Flesh

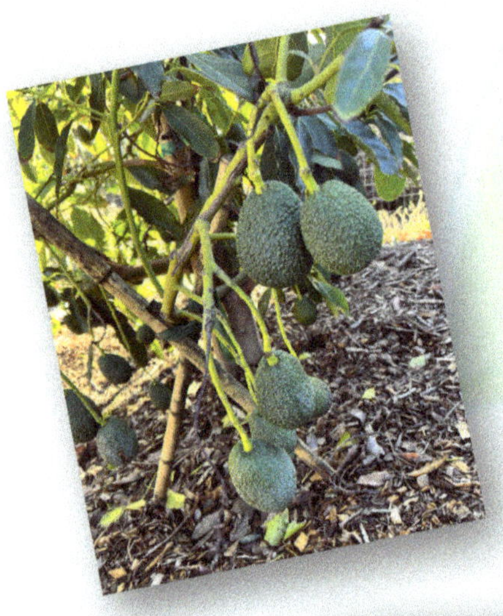

Avocados are a healthy fruit with oils that are very good for your eyes, vision, and skin.

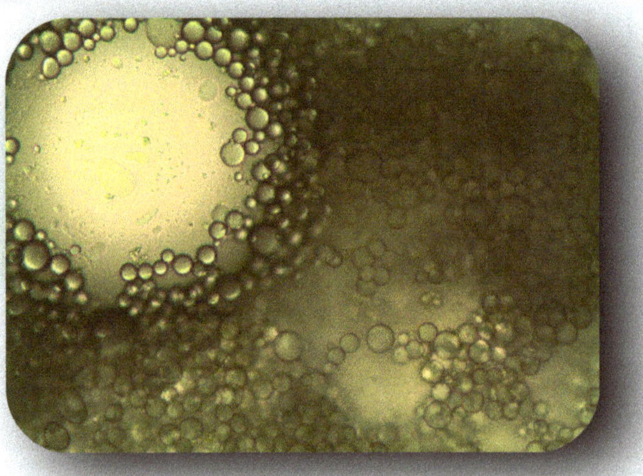

Avocado Flesh, 200x, unstained, flattened. An avocado's flesh has a mushy and oily texture. The large amount of circular drips are oils within the flesh. The texture makes it perfect for spreading and mashing.

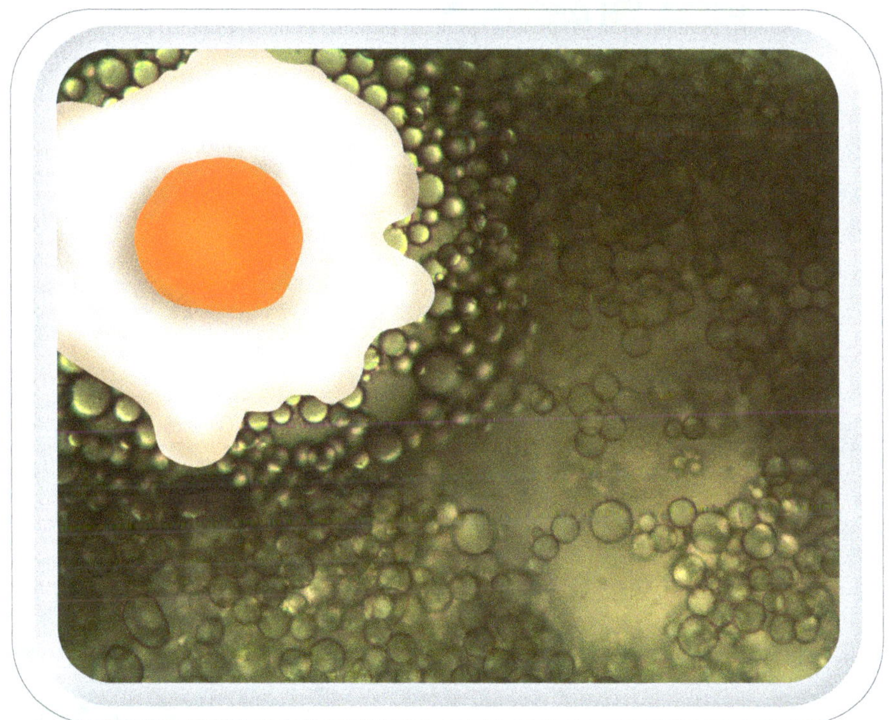

As you can see when coloring in some areas, this can look like a sunny side up egg; the soft yolk will drip down once poked by a fork. Can you think about the past of this egg? All the way from a chicken to your table, this dish can be accompanied by cereal, which you will see later on.

Banana Stem

Natural bananas are actually filled with seeds. But over time, they were bred to be what we know as bananas today!

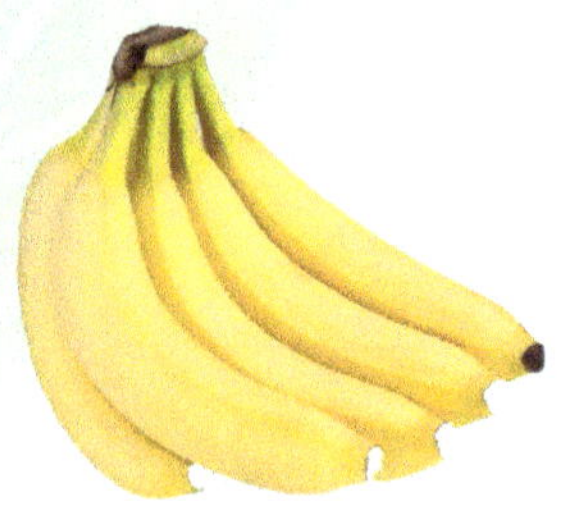

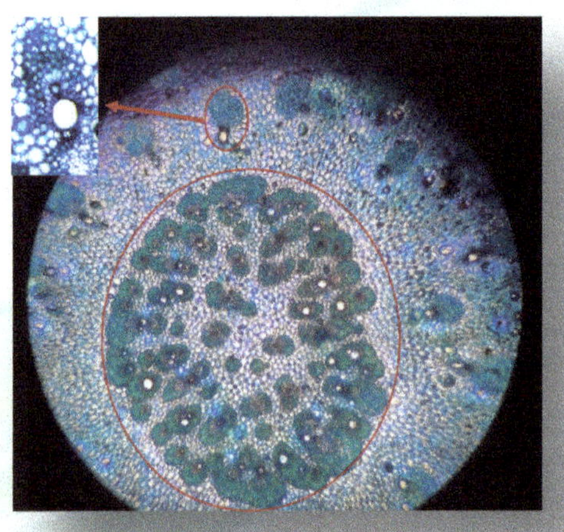

Banana Stem, 40x, 1% Toluidine Blue O. stained, cross section.

The darker blue areas in this image—including the clustered circular items in the central area (within the big red circle) and the scattered items located in the periphery of the stem (the smaller red circle)—are vascular bundles. Each vascular bundle unit is made of a vascular bundle sheath, phloem and xylem (the transparent bubble within each unit; see inserted upper left image). The clear areas are the ground tissues that provide support.

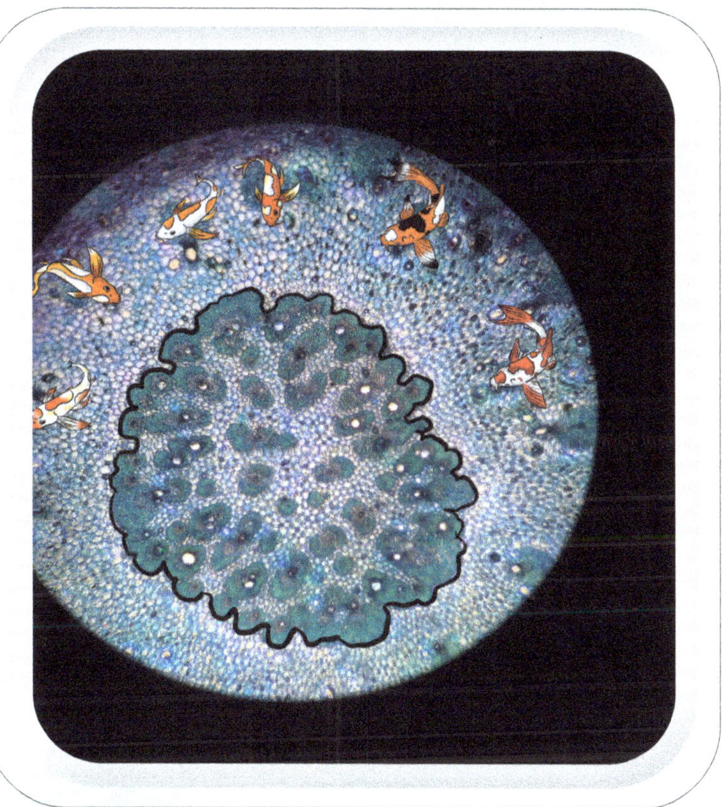

This also looks like a pond full of koi fish swimming around a rock. Koi fish are well known for their colorful skin and decorative purposes, and seen quite often in Asia.

Basil Leaf

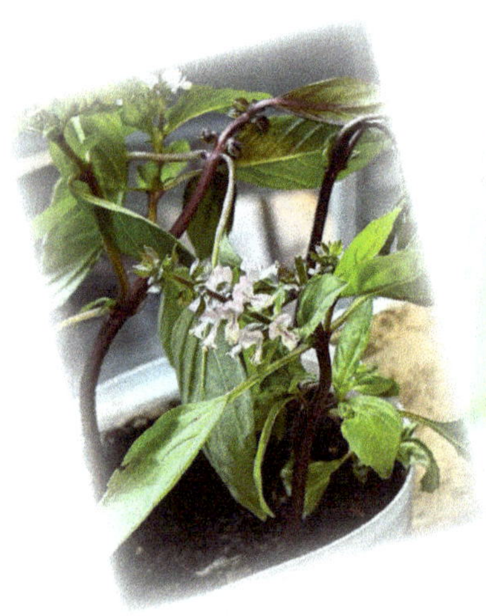

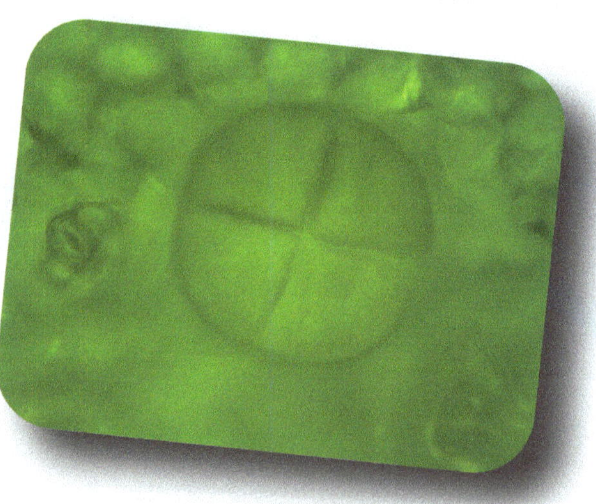

Basil Leaf Top Surface, 400x, unstained, uncut. *The first thing that we noticed about this leaf is the large circular shape divided by quarters in the leaf next to the stomata on the left. Notice the size difference between them. This has never been observed on any other leaf in this book.*

This is a picture of a rainy spring scene. Spring is a season where new plants and flowers grow. Two people running through a spring shower. The person with the umbrella is running towards the person without it, hoping to share sanctuary with him.

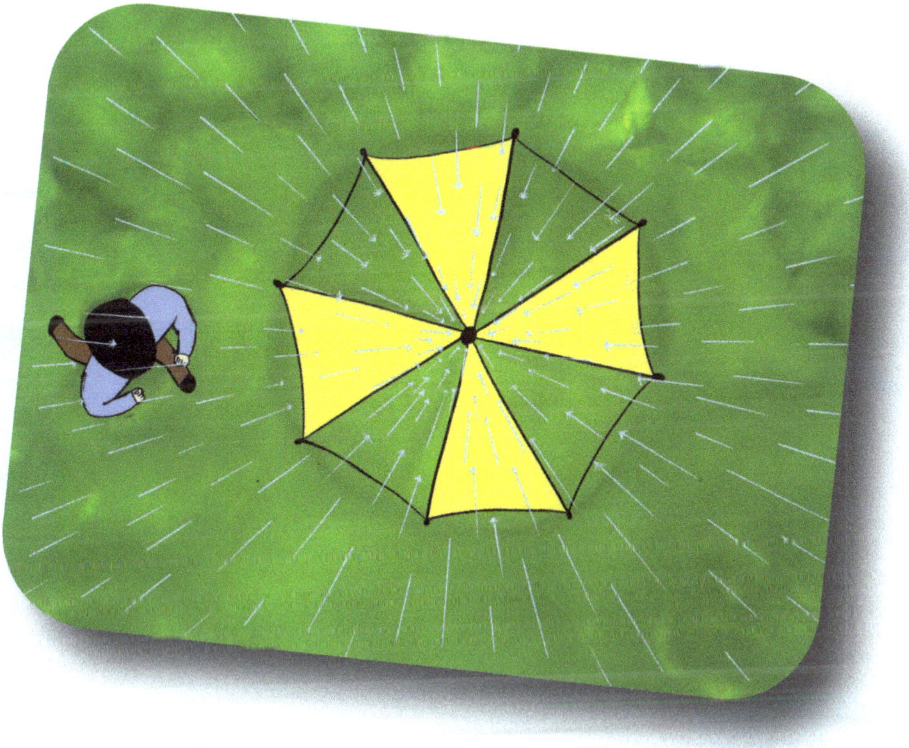

Bean Sprout Stem

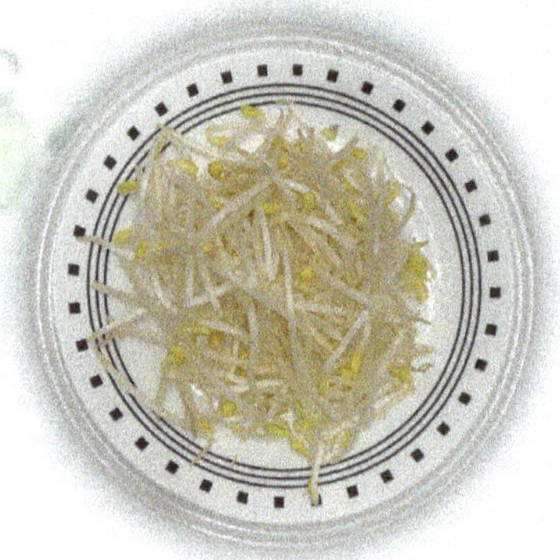

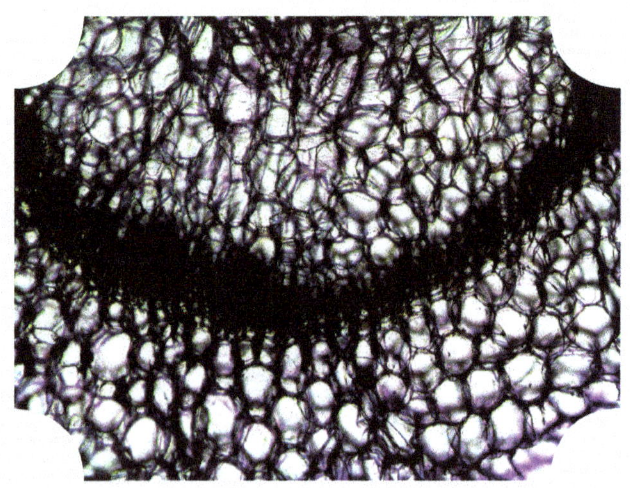

Bean Sprout Stem, 40X, 1% Toluidine Blue O stained, **cross section**. *In this magnification, one can see large, circular-structure cells (light area) around the phenolic bodies (dark area in the middle). Phenolic bodies are embedded in a ring in the middle of the stem.*

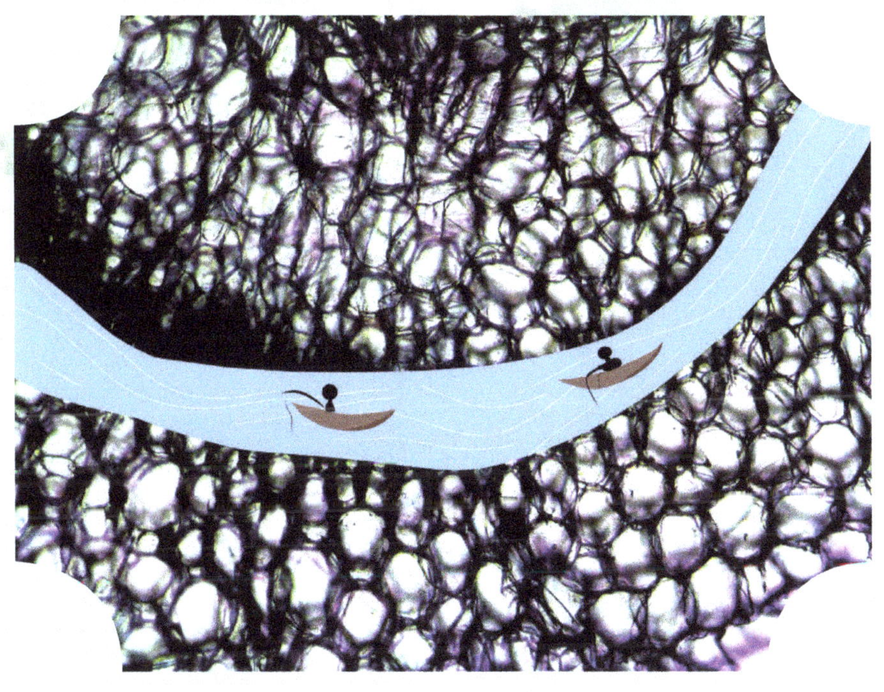

Spring had just arrived, bringing with it an abundance of fresh fish, and attracting many fishermen. They had come from an icy winter, and were ready to start providing for their families. The river was created from a mountain stream, flowing into the ocean. One can see through the crystal-clear waters as if they were glass.

Celery Stem

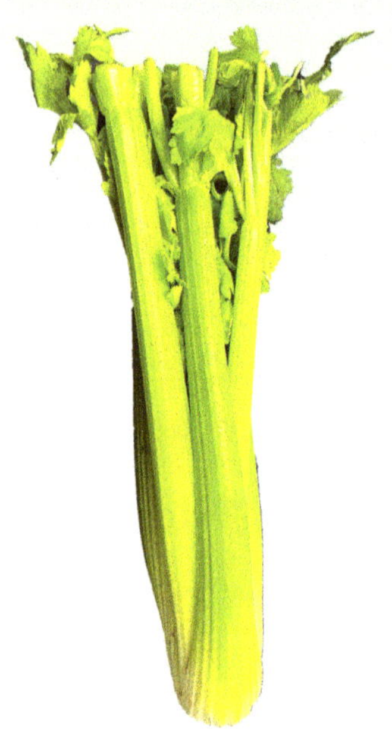 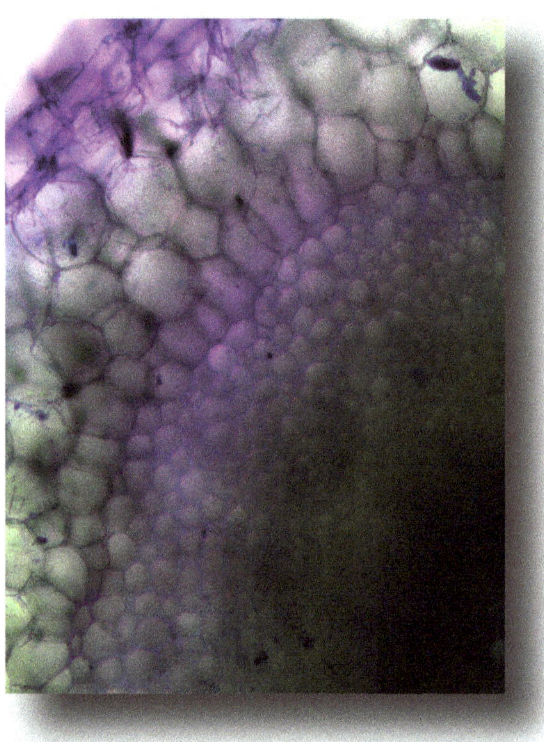

Celery Stem, 100X, 1% Toluidine Blue O. stained, cross section. *The celery is divided into a few layers. The dark purple at the upper left edge of the image is the epidermis layer (a hard layer of the plant used to protect it), and the second layer is the cortex, mainly made of large cells. The rest of the layers (the bottom right edge of the image) are the phloem of a vascular bundle. Look closely!*

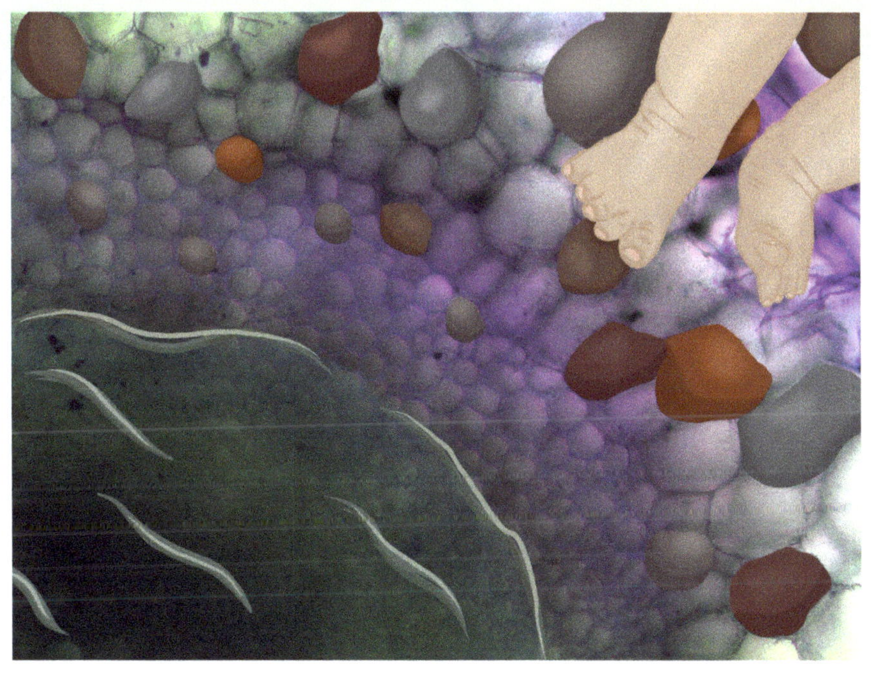

A little baby waddles across the pebble beach, as the destination of her chubby feet is the cool, refreshing water. The thought of the water makes her tiny toes tingle and the pebbles make her feet feel rough and slightly sting. But still, she was intrigued by the colorful pebbles, forgot her mission, and squats down to pick one up...

Cucumber

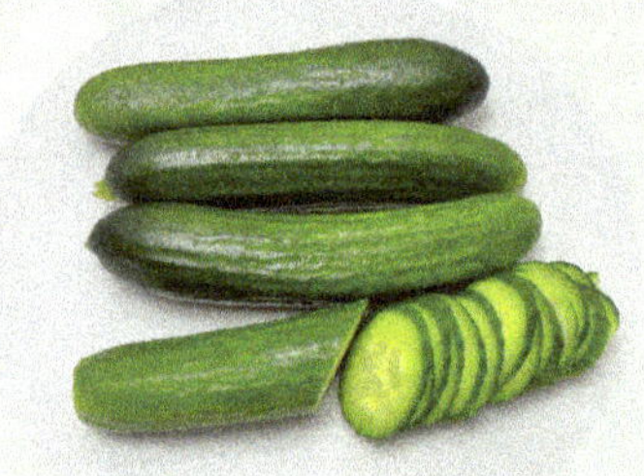

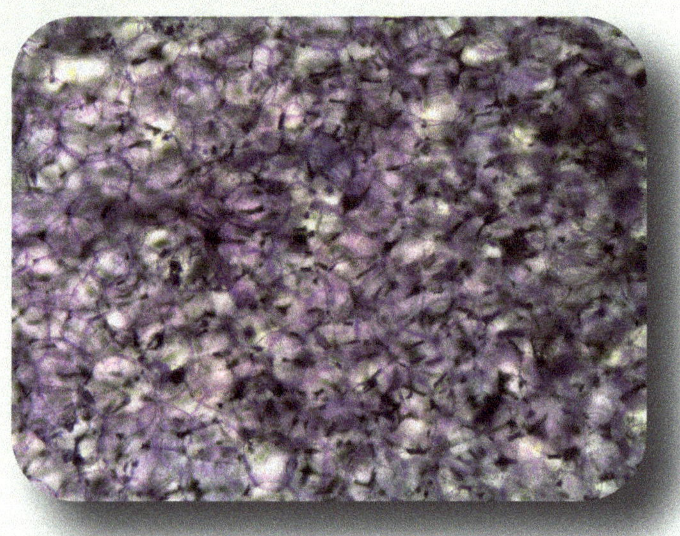

Cucumber, 40X, 1% Toluidine Blue O. stained, cross section. In this magnification, you can see the crowded purple thin-walled cells. The cells are overlaying each other. Unfortunately, the black dots were some unclean areas that were trapped between cells while staining with the Toluidine Blue dye.

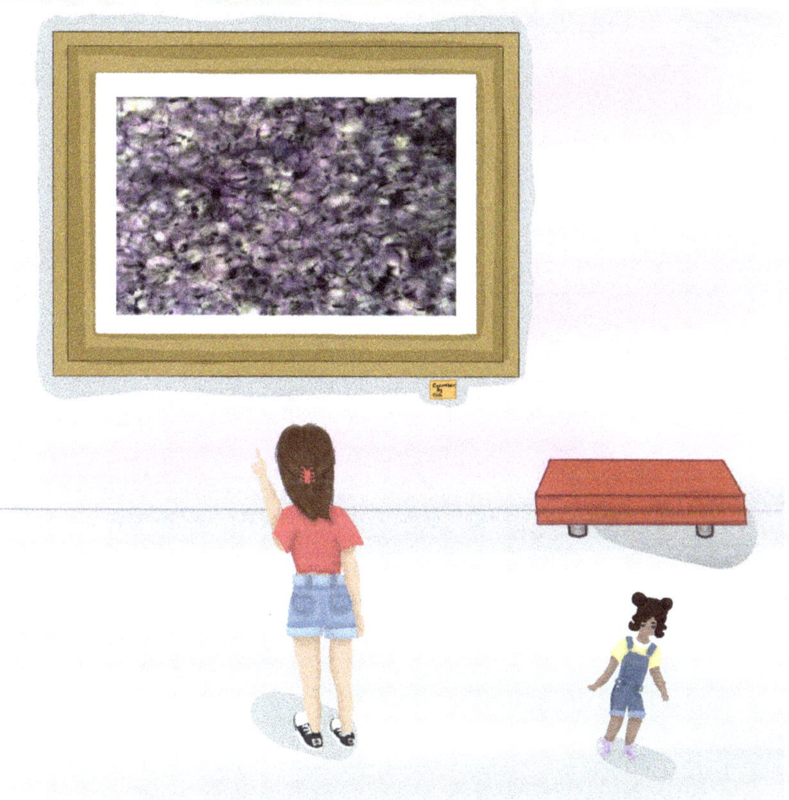

A little girl's sneakers squeak as she runs across the shiny gallery floor, while another girl admires the unique art piece hanging on the wall. What looks like an abstract art piece is actually a cucumber underneath a microscope. She wonders to herself: is it art or science?

Guava Flesh

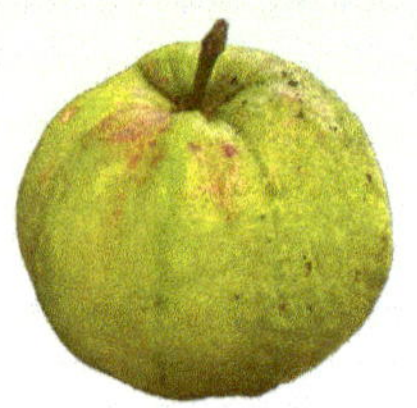

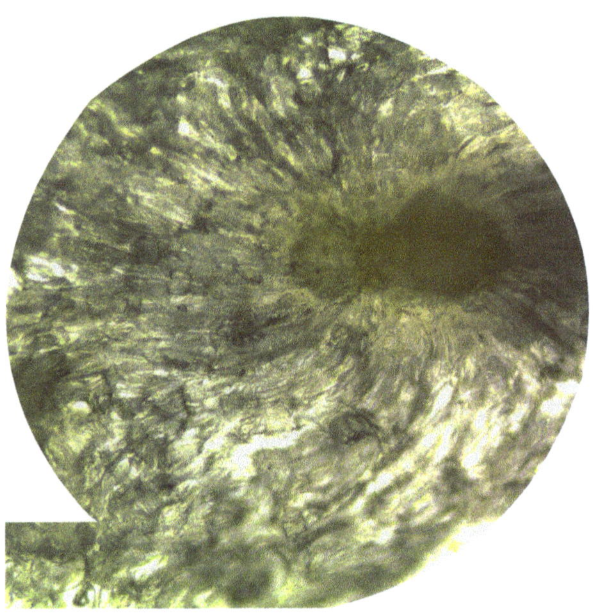

Guava Fruit Flesh, 40x, unstained, cross section. In the middle of this picture, a darker peanut shape can be seen. It is made of coarse particles. The things surrounding it are made of thinner particles. Together, it gives the rough texture it is known for today. In this magnification level, the inside of the cells cannot be observed. You should experiment sometime on your own!

As you can see, it looks like a strong wave in the ocean. So when you add figures, it can look like two courageous surfers that are surfing against the strong wave. Surfing is a fun water sport that can be enjoyed all year around, but is mainly enjoyed in the humid summer season.

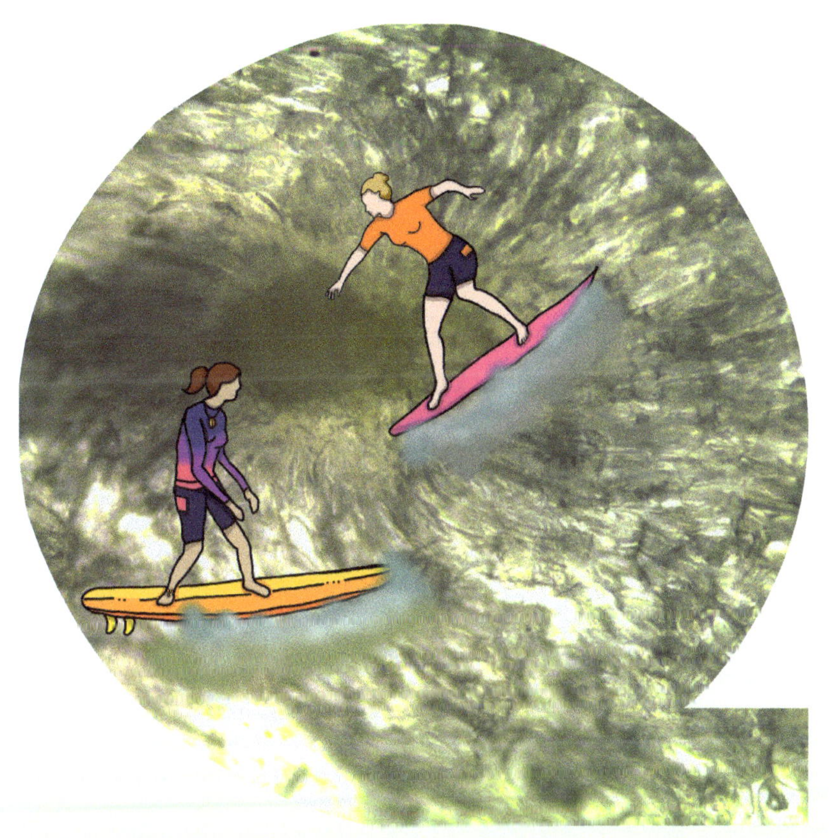

Mushroom Gill

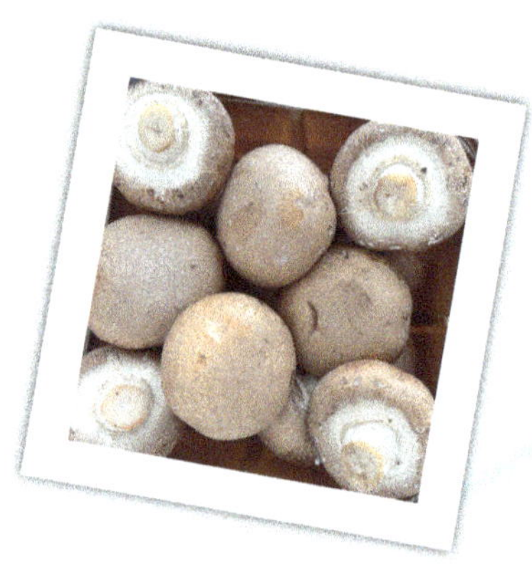

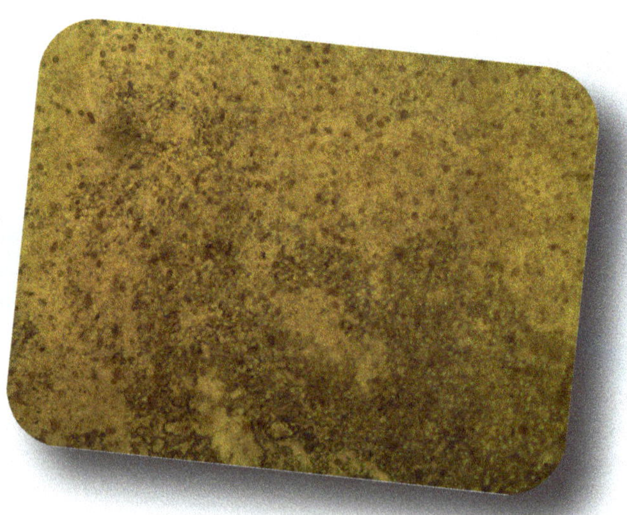

Mushroom Gill, 100x, unstained, cross section. *Mushroom is a fungus—meaning a whole bunch of spores can be observed on its body. These spores are like the seeds of the mushroom, helping the plant reproduce.*

A pirate map to the mythical Isles of Conquest. Legend says that a pirate once buried all his treasure on the "X" mark. Now, whoever can sail through all the treacherous natural barriers can finally claim the long lost treasure.

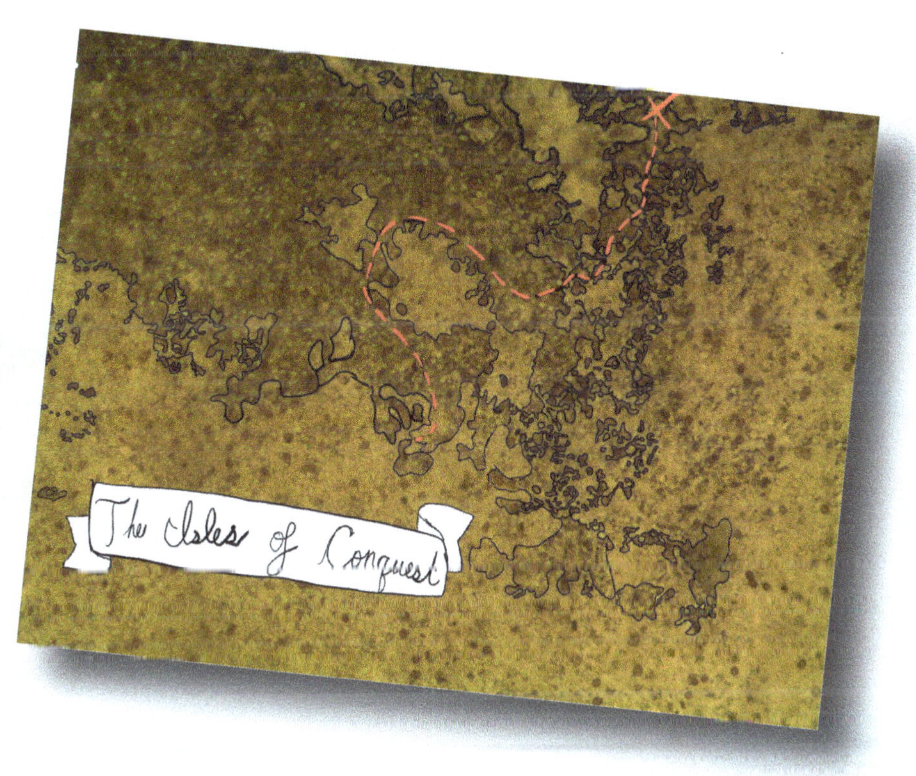

Okra Seed

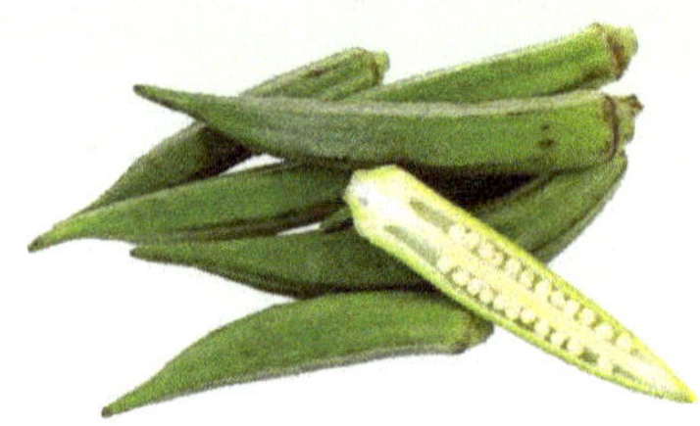

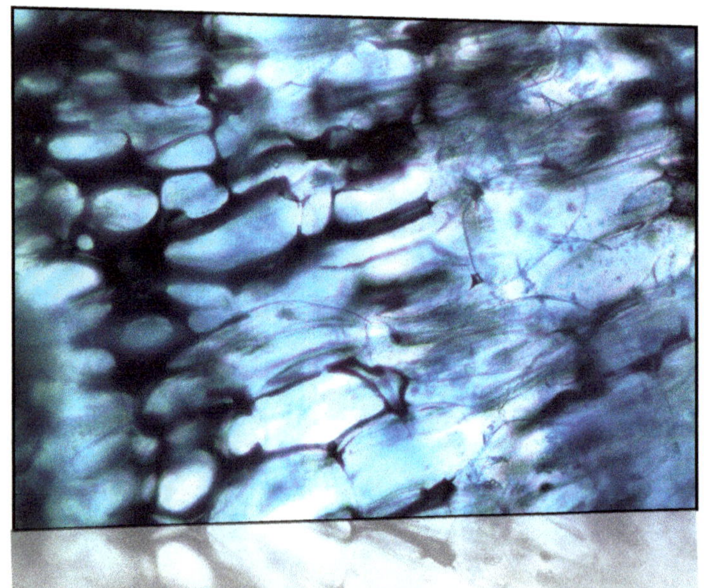

Okra Seed, 100x, 1% Toluidine Blue O. stained, cross section. *The okra seed is composed of a wide variety of cells of different shapes and sizes. Notice the interesting 'pattern' of the cells, due to the okra's unusual texture. It usually has a bit of a slimy feel, which is the reason for the cells' amorphous shape.*

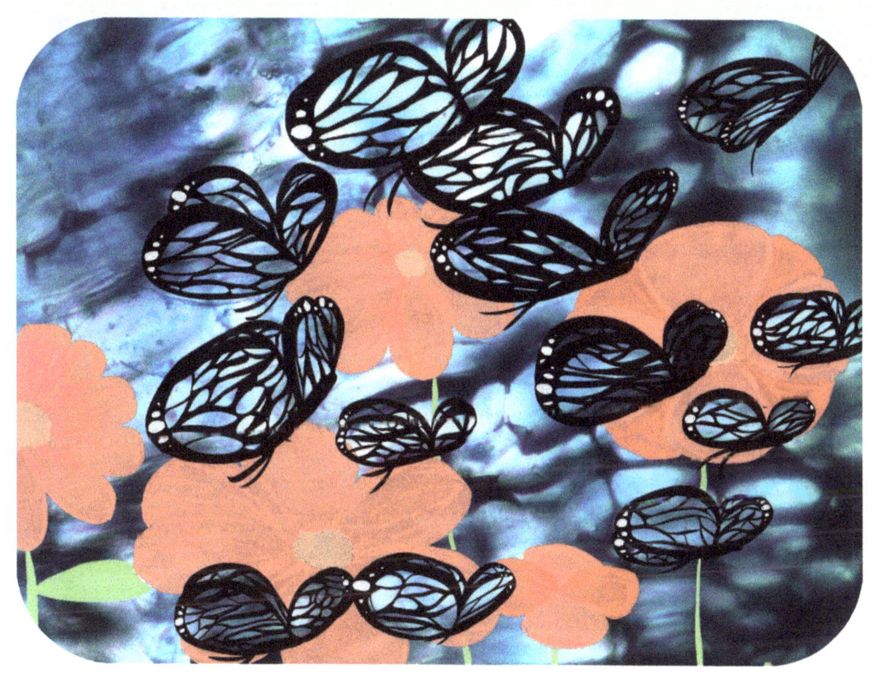

It's a beautiful day, the Blue Morpho butterflies fly across the land and pollinate wildflowers in their path. The pattern of the Okra seed cells creates the texture of the magnificent blue morpho butterflies gathering around and pollinating the colorful plants. Tt is truly an amazing sight.

Onion Skin

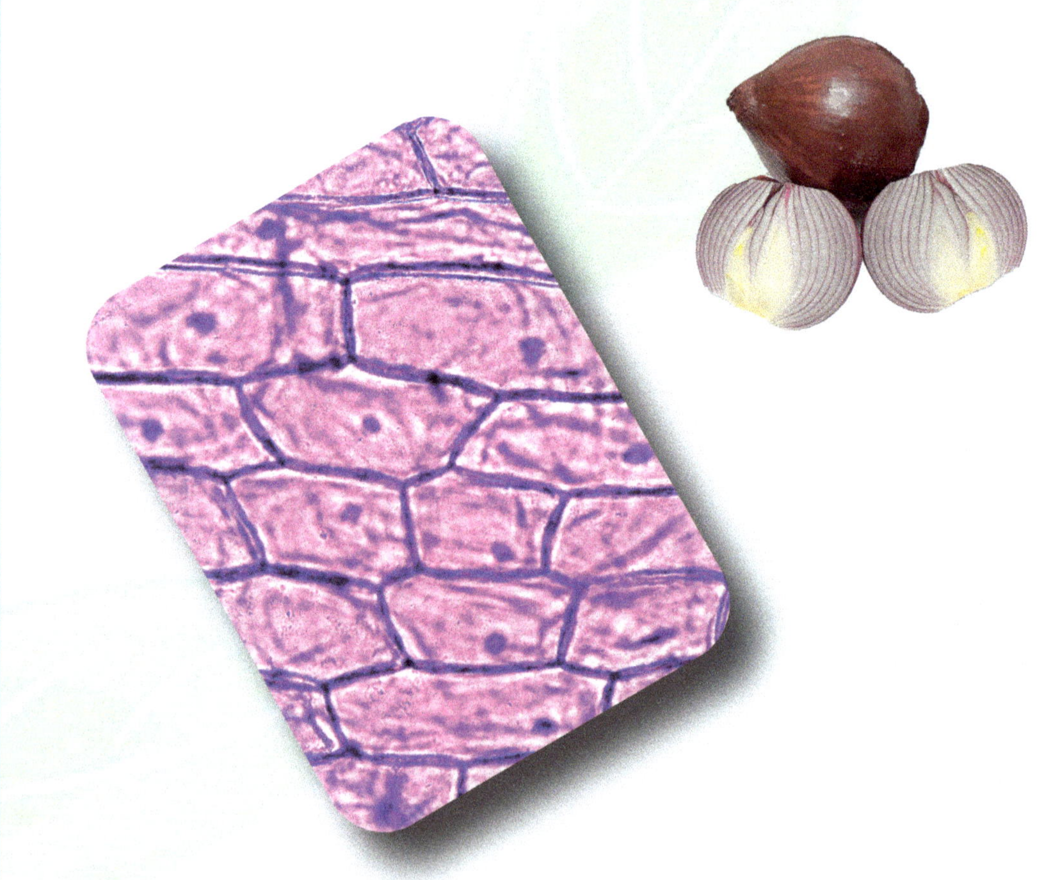

Red Onion Skin, 100x, unstained, peeled. *This is a micro-scopic image of a piece of onion skin. It can be observed to have a square structure (which is very common in plants). As you can see, each onion cell has a small dot in the middle. That small dot is its nucleus.*

As you can see when observing this image, the pattern makes it look like a brick wall. When adding a few simple adjustments outside of the image, it can look like a nice backyard on a warm, humid summer day. See the cute ginger cat snoozing on the brick wall? It has forgotten all its fears, and is certainly not remembering that it is stuck!

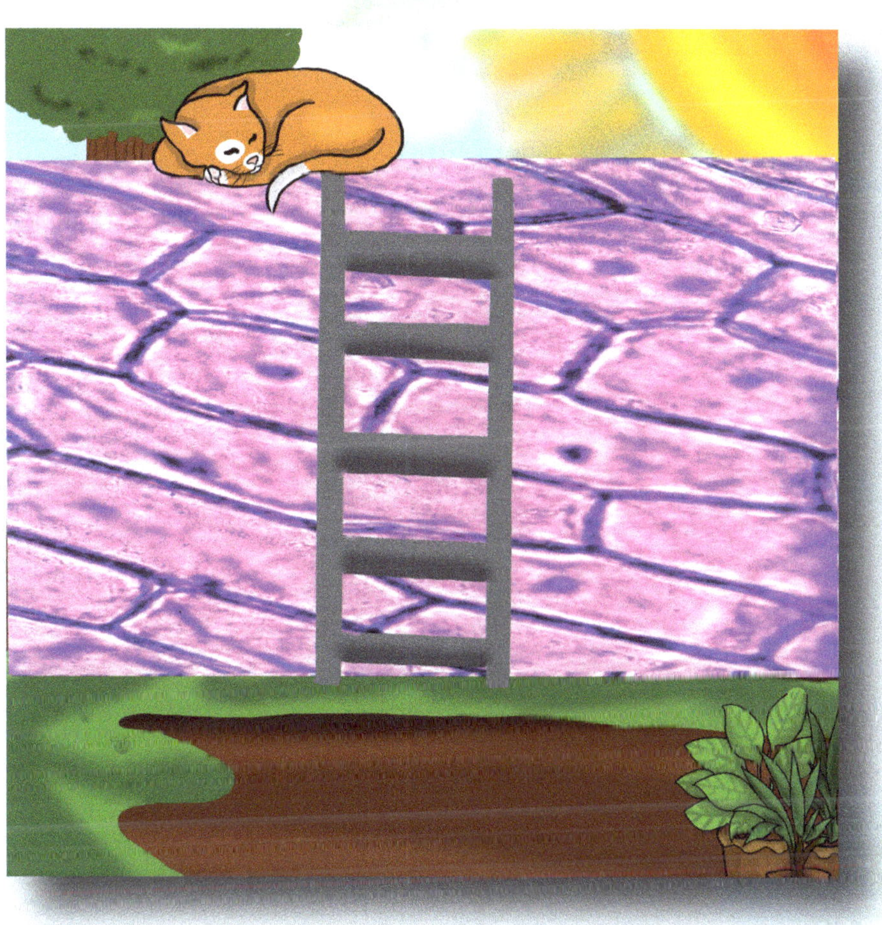

Orange Bell Pepper

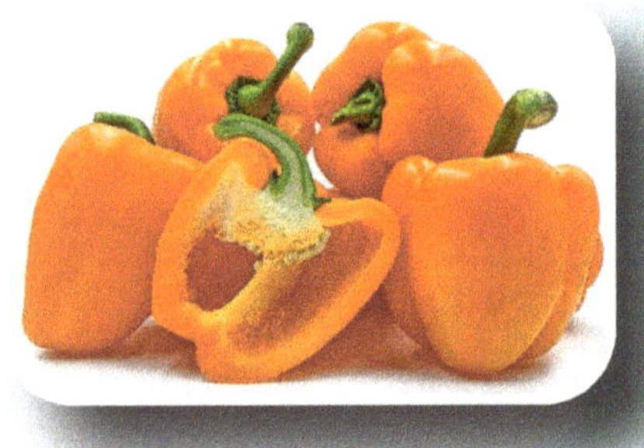

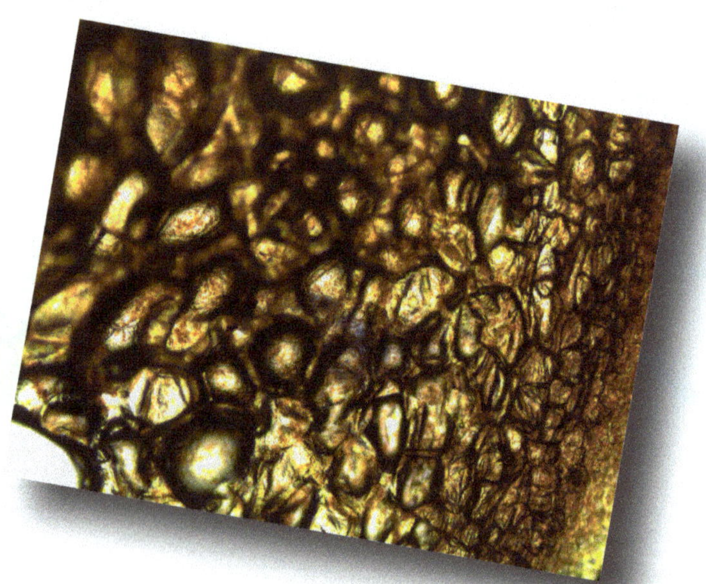

Orange Bell Pepper, 40X, Iodine stained, cross section. *The golden nugget-like shapes are cells. The tiny orange spots are chromoplasts, which produce and store carotenoid pigments in flowers and fruits. Carotenoid pigments are bright red, yellow, and orange colors.*

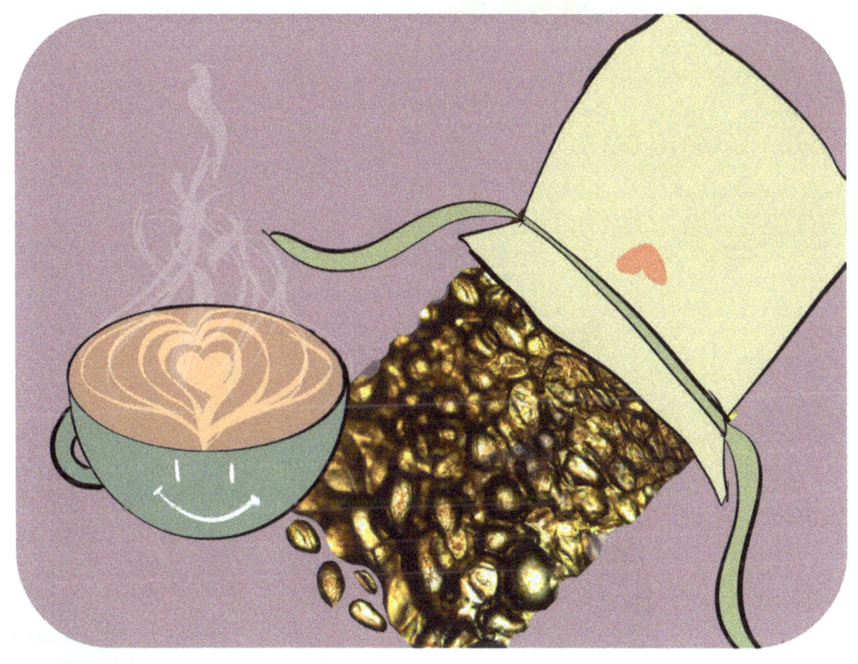

What's better than a cozy cup of coffee with heart-swirled foam in the morning? The creamy taste is to die for, with the nice earthy kick of some coffee made from fresh coffee beans. A home-brewed cappuccino is an amazing thing to wake up to, especially with the freshest organic coffee beans.

Potato

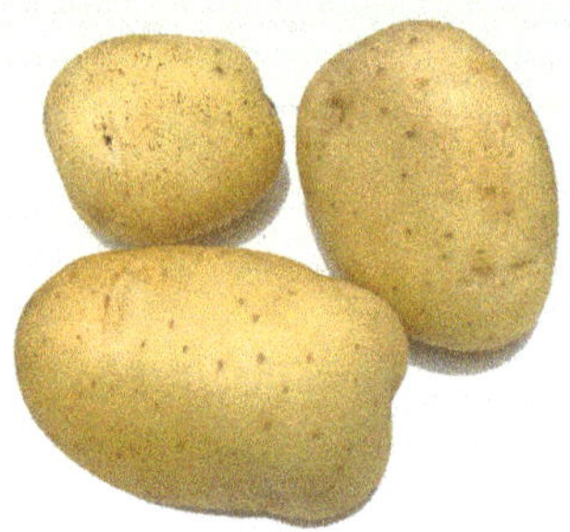

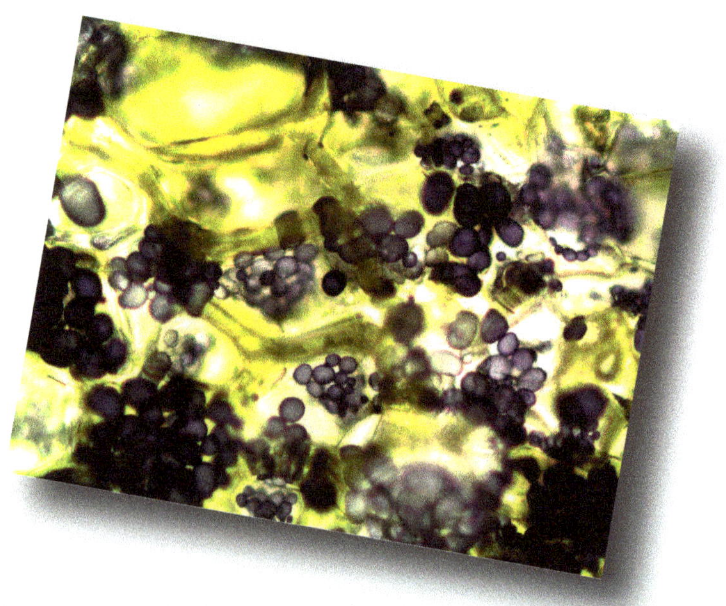

Potato Flesh, 100x, iodine stained, cross section. This image can be observed to have granules inside the cells. The yellow parts are the cells, and the darker outlines are the cell wall. The purple bubble-like clusters are a reaction from iodine and starch. Starch turns purple due to direct exposure to Iodine via chemical reactions.

If you add a stem and leaves, this can look like a cluster of sweet and juicy grapes, which can be enjoyed and harvested in the crisp autumn season and weather.

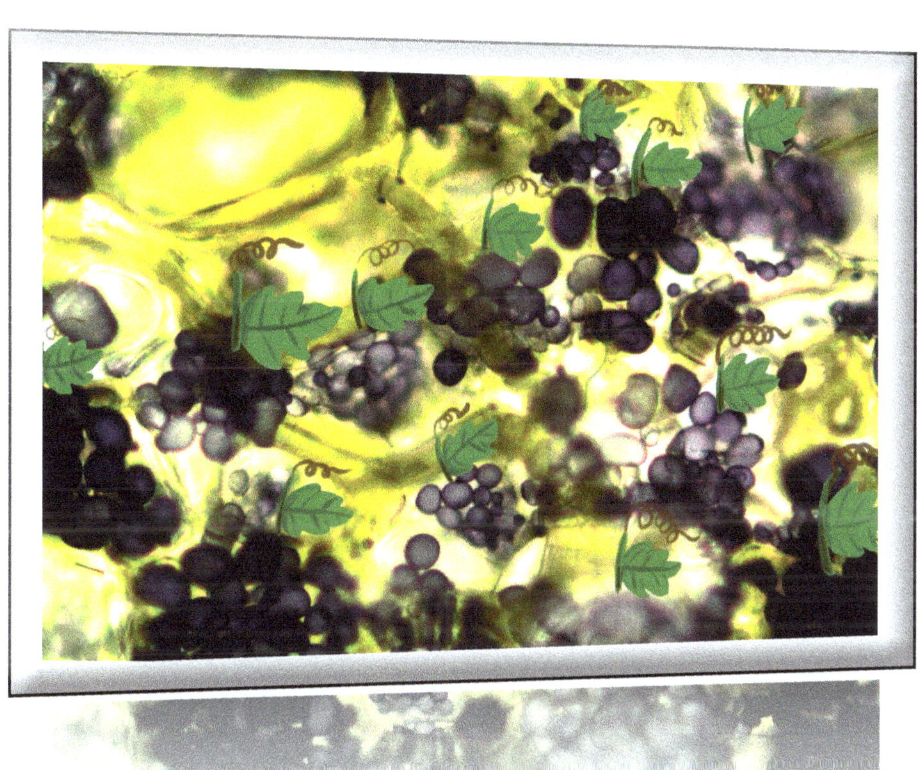

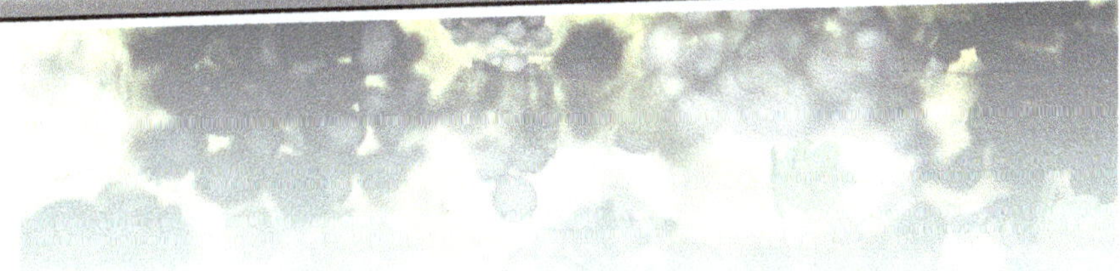

Purple Cauliflower

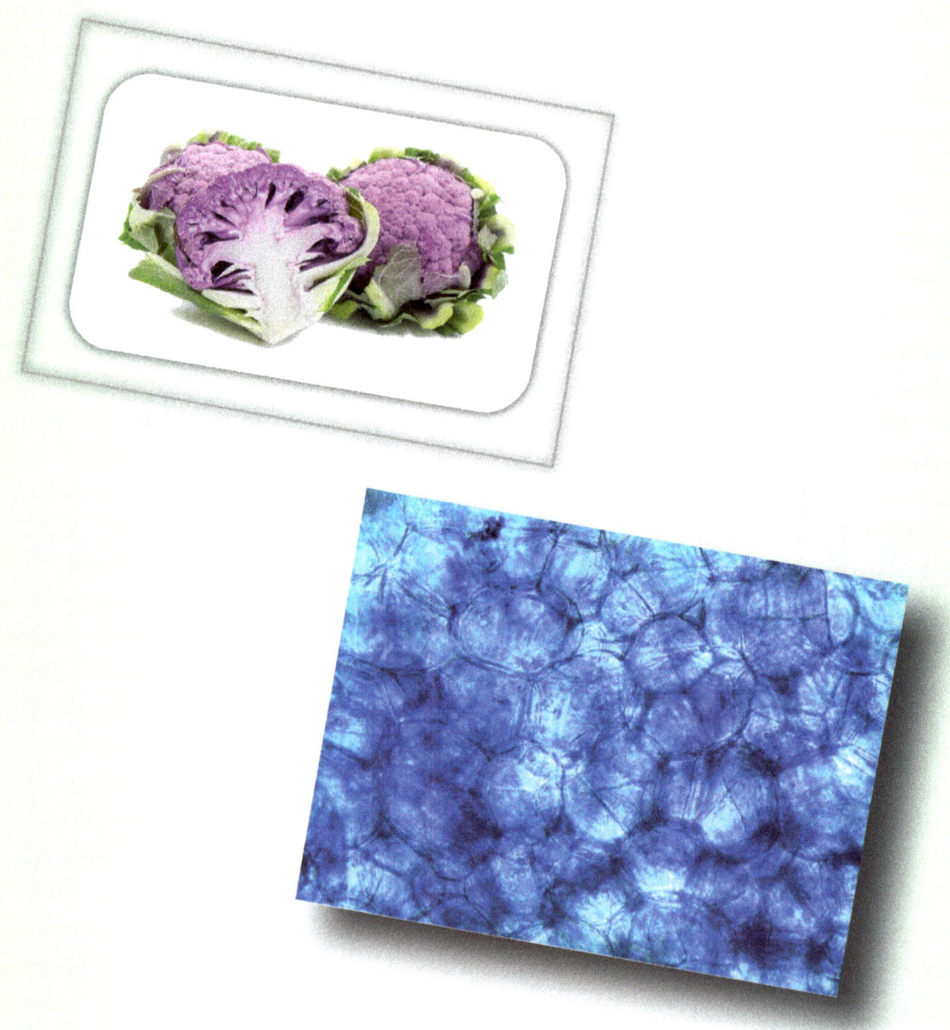

Purple Cauliflower, 200X, Blue ink stained, cross section. *The thin walled cells of the purple cauliflower are very compact, almost having no space between them. The bubble-resembling shapes are what help the cauliflower hold together and gather nutrients.*

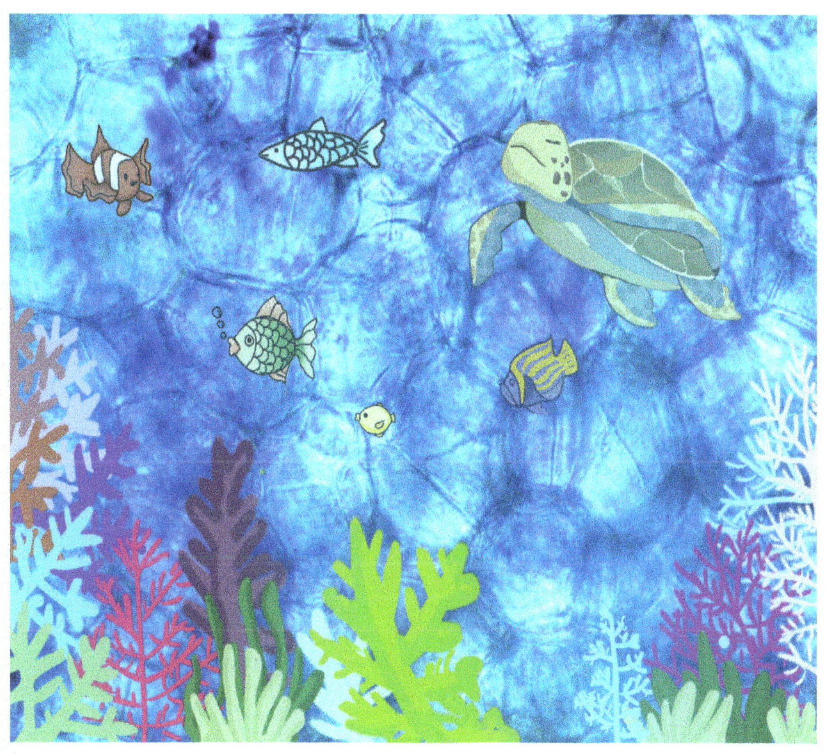

A turtle glides across the glassy water, gazing at the big bubbles. Fish swim around and explore their ocean home. Colorful coral dances across the sandy sea floor, like a rainbow that stretches across the sky. Even though it's invisible to the naked eye, millions of little organisms live around the coral to hide from predators. Something else invisible is the plankton that drifts with the current. This is the underwater kingdom.

Red Cactus Pear Skin

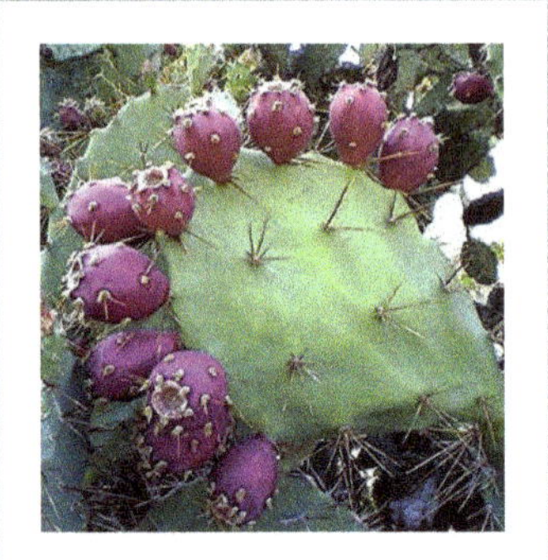

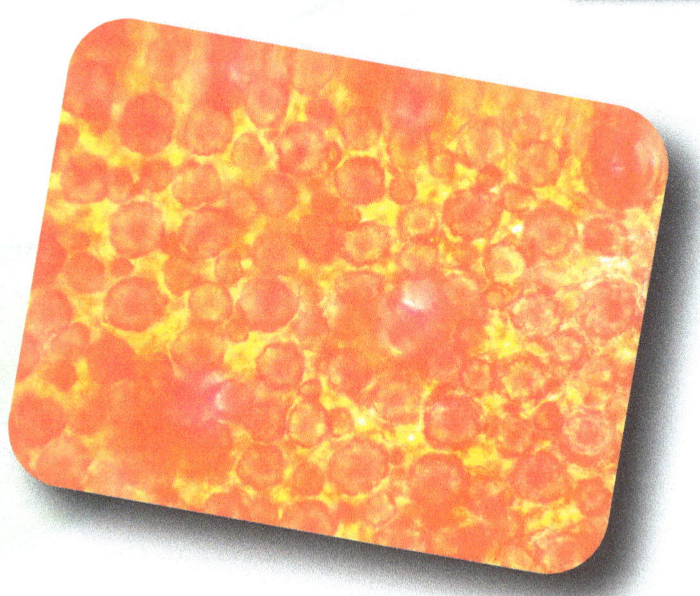

Red Cactus Pear Skin, 200X, unstained, peeled. *The prominent round cells are very warm shades, including reds, oranges, and yellows. The especially red dots in the middle of the cells are the cell nuclei, which stores the plant's hereditary material (used to reproduce).*

Lunar New Year is a fun and festive holiday where people celebrate by eating good food and stringing up lanterns. Lanterns are there to commemorate a Chinese myth about a dragon who terrorized humans but was afraid of the color red. The food that is generally eaten includes sweet rice balls, spring rolls, dumplings, and more! It truly is a fun event.

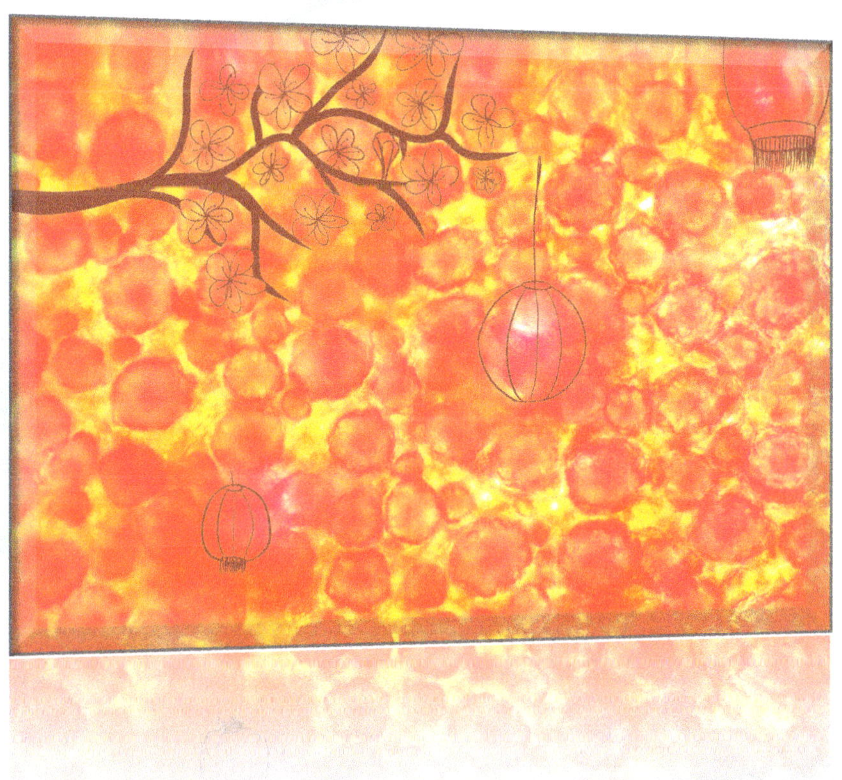

Spinach Leaf

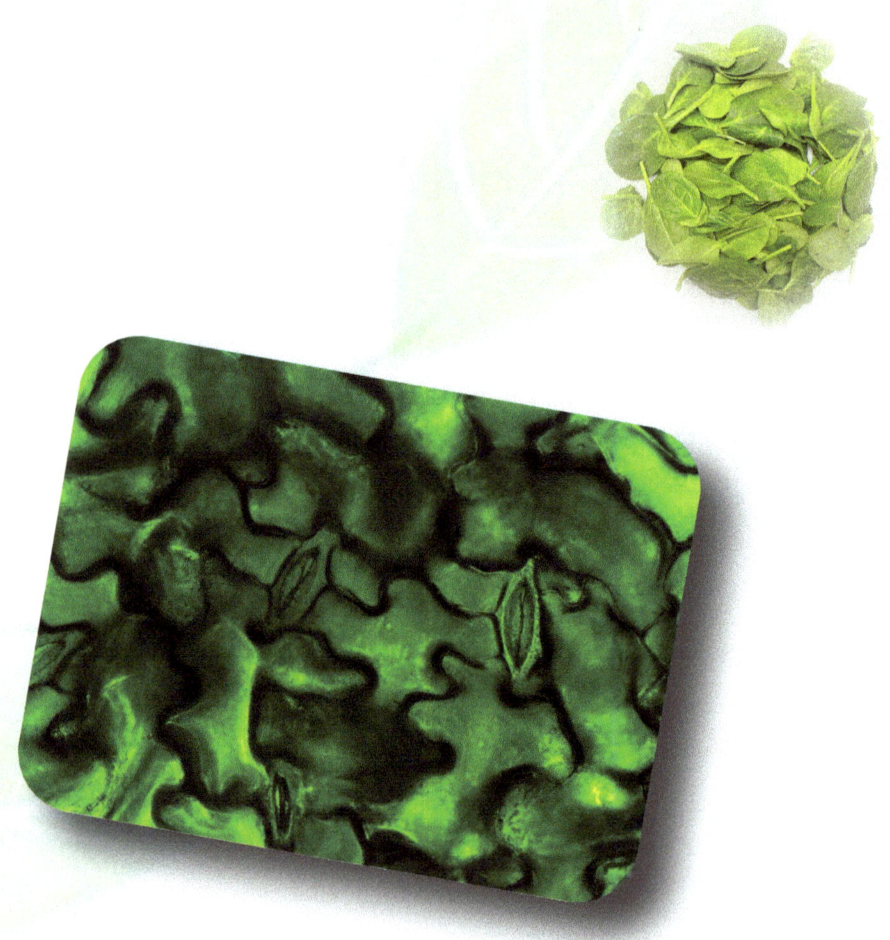

Spinach Leaf, 200X, unstained, *uncut*. The coffee bean shapes are stomas (also called stomatas or stomates. How many can you see in this picture?) They are pores that control the rate of gas exchange for photosynthesis. The squiggly lines are cells. The amorphous shapes are used for the plant's benefit in receiving nutrients.

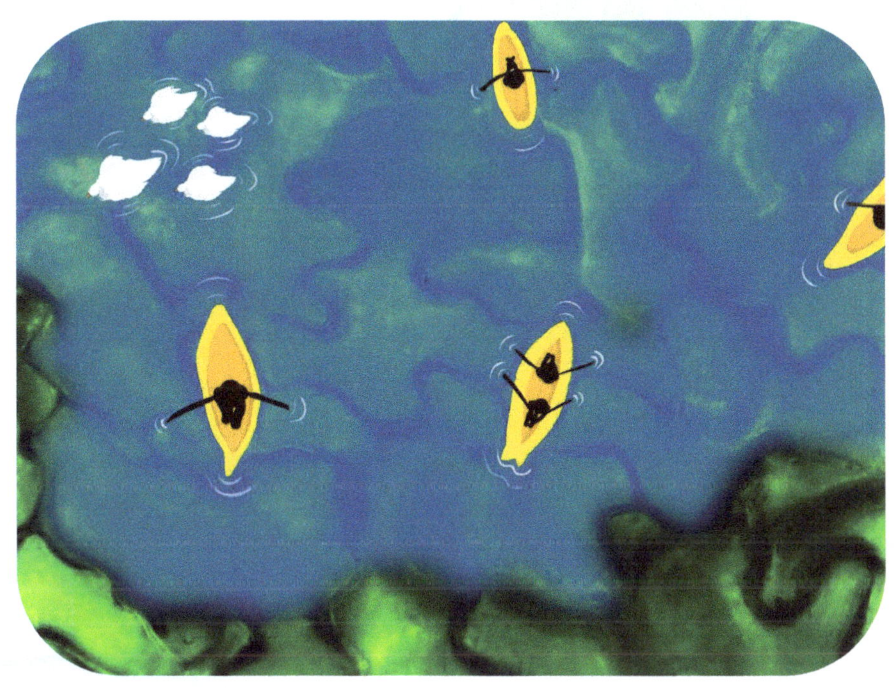

It's spring; the shore has turned emerald green. The ice has melted into clear water, so clear that you can see the bottom of the pond. Swans are peacefully swimming off the shoreline. It's the perfect time to kayak! Either with friends or by yourself, kayaking is a fun sport enjoyed by people from all around the world. Better watch out! or you might just splash into the icy water.

Part B

Flowers and Leaves

Aquarium Algae

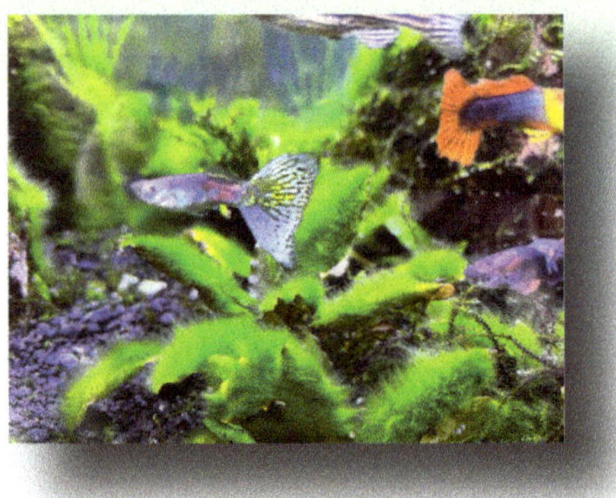

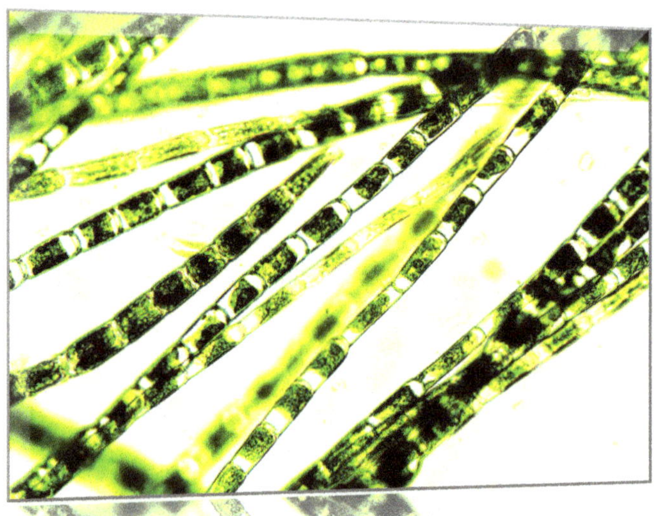

Aquarium Algae, 200X, unstained, uncut. *Each strand is an individual plant, part of a clump of algae. Each section of a strand is an individual cell. The algae's green areas are chlorophyll, which is used to absorb sunlight.*

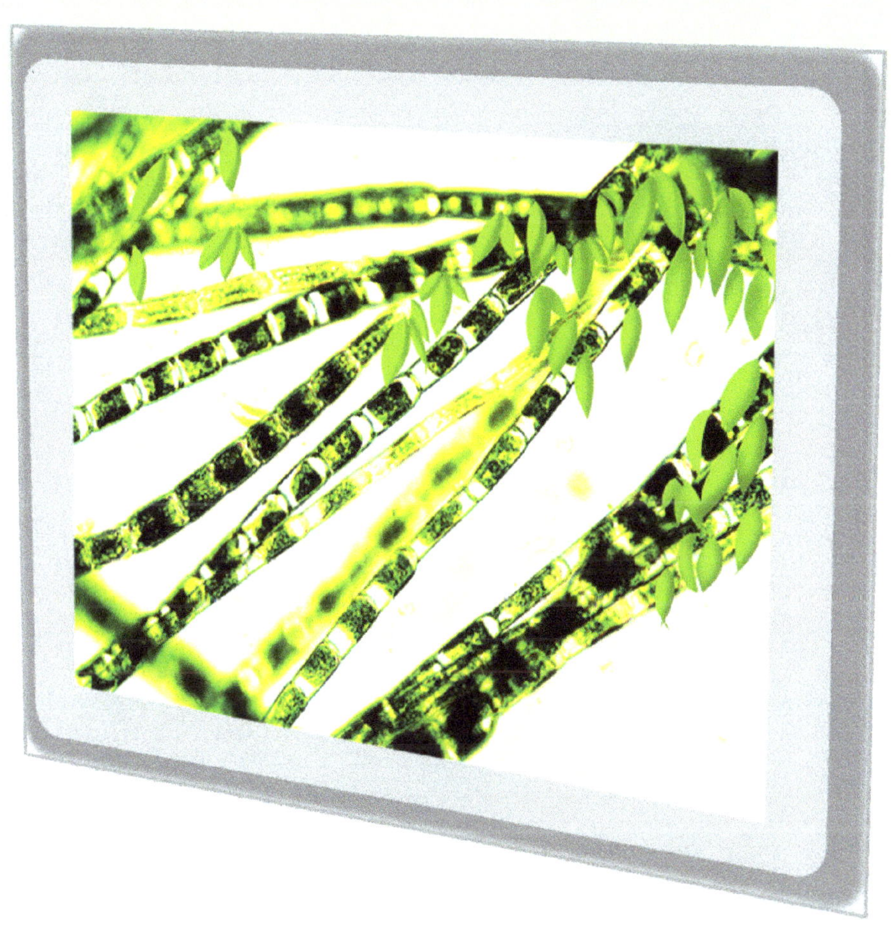

If leaves are added, it can be used as a beautiful patch of bamboo in the springtime. Bamboo is generally a plant that grows very fast in spring, and can be a direct comparison to how quickly a child grows over a short period of time.

Aquarium Moss

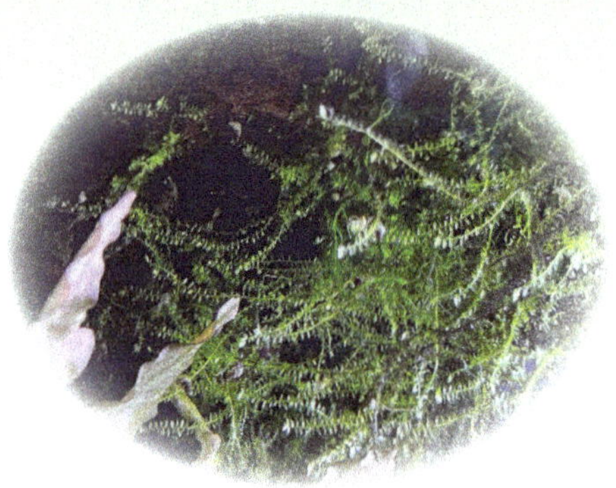

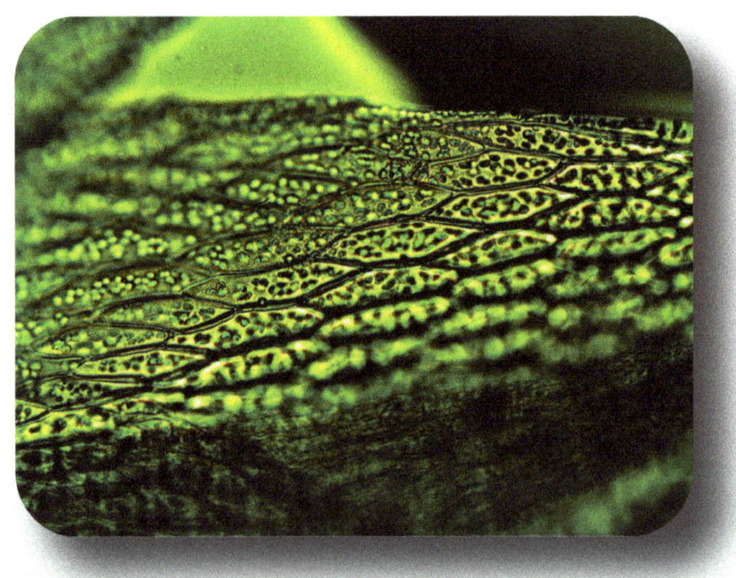

Aquarium Moss, 200X, unstained, uncut. *Moss under a microscope is observed to have tightly packed hexagon grids, which are the cells. The dots inside of the hexagon-shaped cells are chlorophyll.*

It also looks like a lake in summer when the sun is shining down upon it. Lotuses are very common around this time, and lily pads are a common habitat of animals such as frogs.

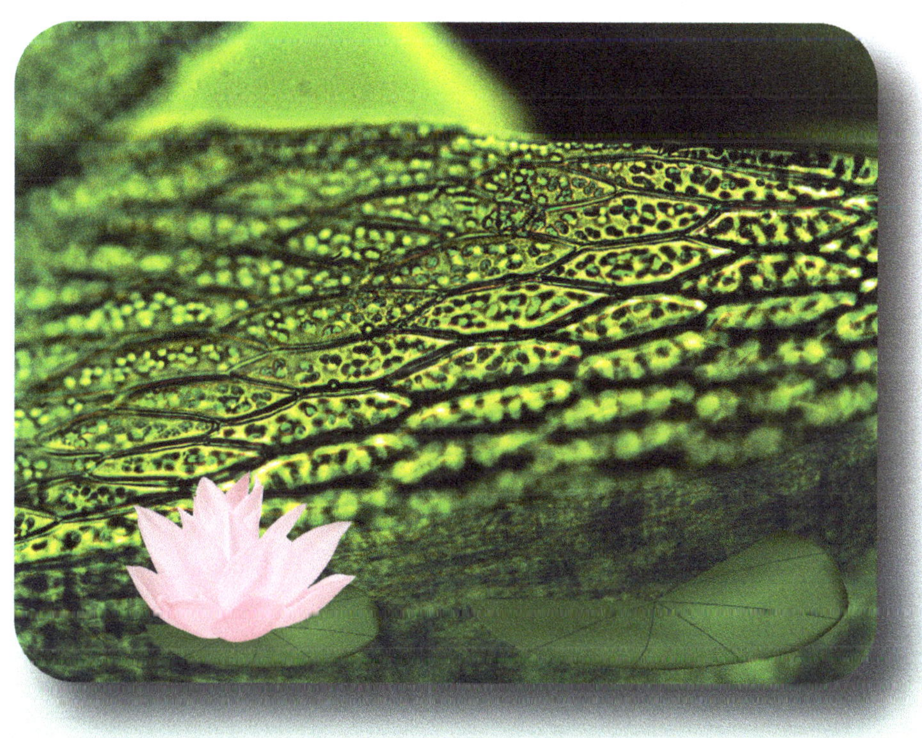

Bamboo Leaf

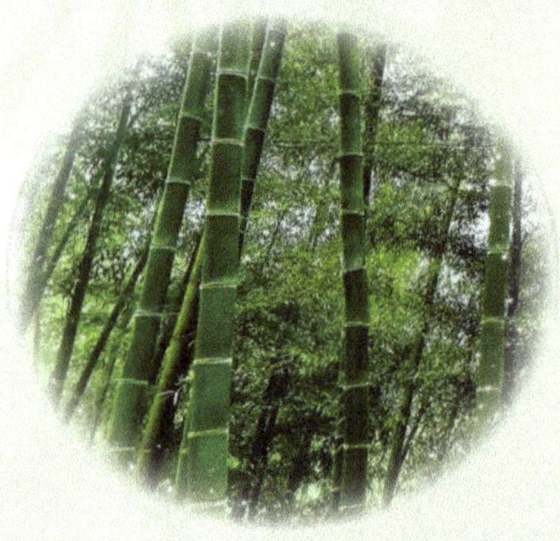

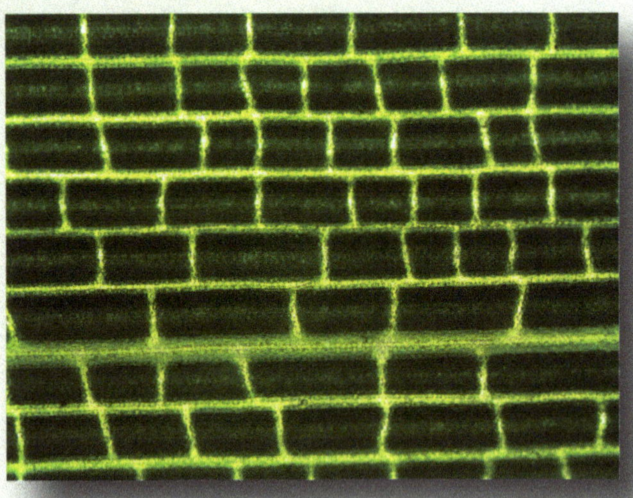

Bamboo Leaf, 40X, unstained, uncut. *Bamboo leaf under a microscope is observed to have tightly packed rectangles, which are the cells, separated by lighter lines. The funny thing is that the cells of bamboo leaves look just like the bamboo stalk!*

The cool night wind sways in the soft lush cherry tree and a little squirrel sleeps soundly in the glowing moonlight. The shovel and bouncy ball are what Mr. Bamboo and his two children play with. Oh! I can hear the distinct meowing from the backyard of Mr. Bamboo's neighbor Mrs. Onion too!

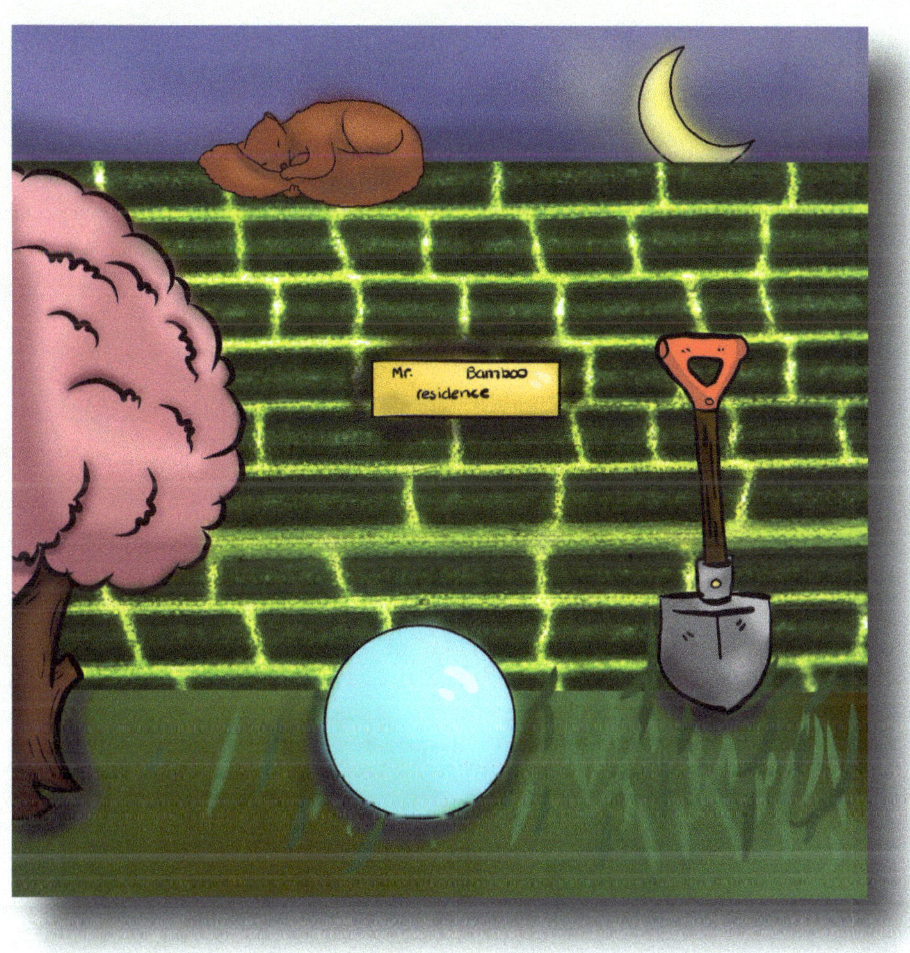

Bristle Grass Leaf

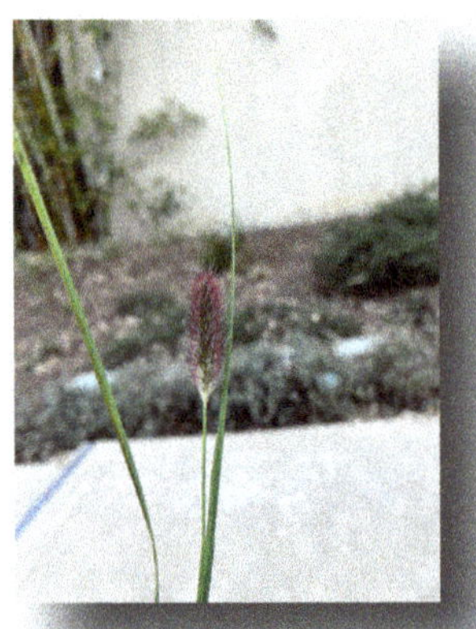

A bristle grass collected on the UCLA campus. It looks like a foxtail.

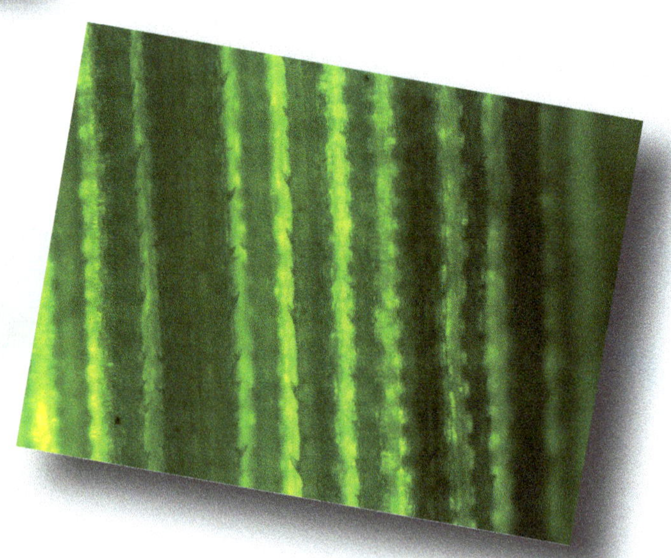

Bristle Grass Leaf, 40x, unstained, uncut. The most notable detail in this picture is the microscopic barbs that all face the same direction on this leaf. The function of these barbs is to hook onto the skin in order to spread the seeds that are at the ends of the plant. This also creates the rough texture of the leaves they are known for.

This also looks like a juicy, mouthwatering watermelon after it's been cut. Watermelon is a type of fruit that generally contains a lot of sugar and water, which makes it a refreshing fruit in hot weather.

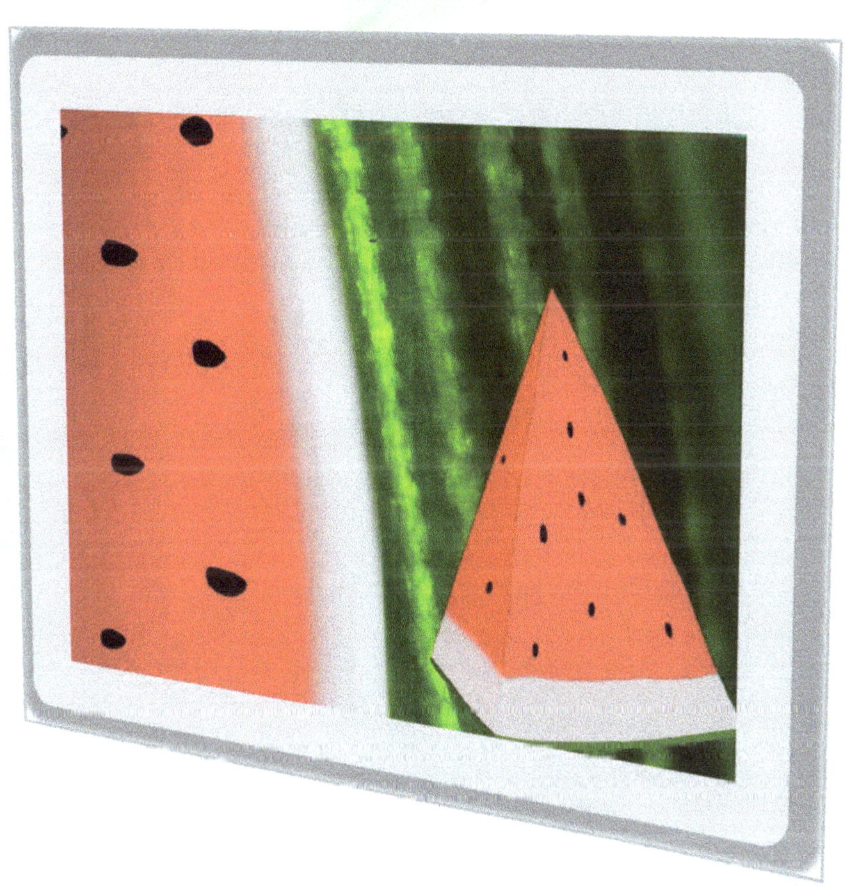

Bougainvillea Flower

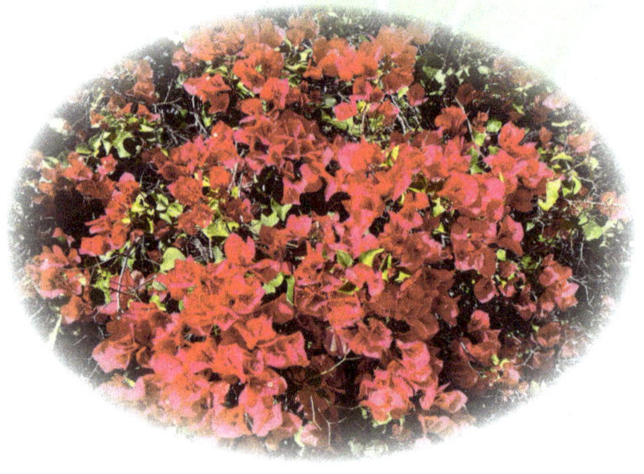

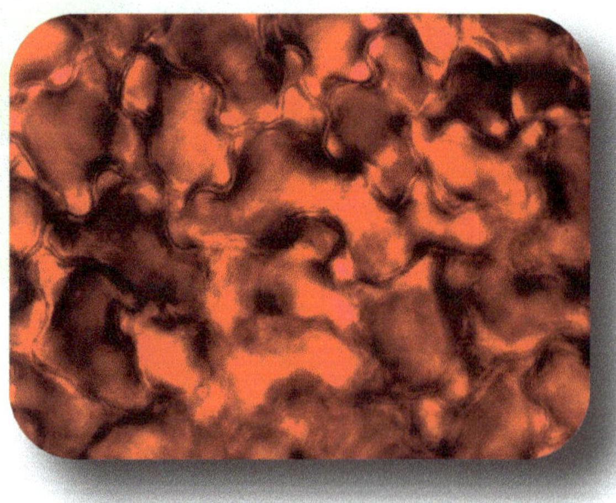

Bougainvillea Flower, 400x, unstained, cross section. *Observed under a microscope, one can see the amorphous structure of the cells. These strange structures help the flower gain the nutrients it needs, along with helping it reproduce.*

When you outline the cell walls, they look like a complex jigsaw puzzle! Jigsaw puzzles are fun challenges that people do to stimulate their minds and cure their boredom. Would you be able to complete this?

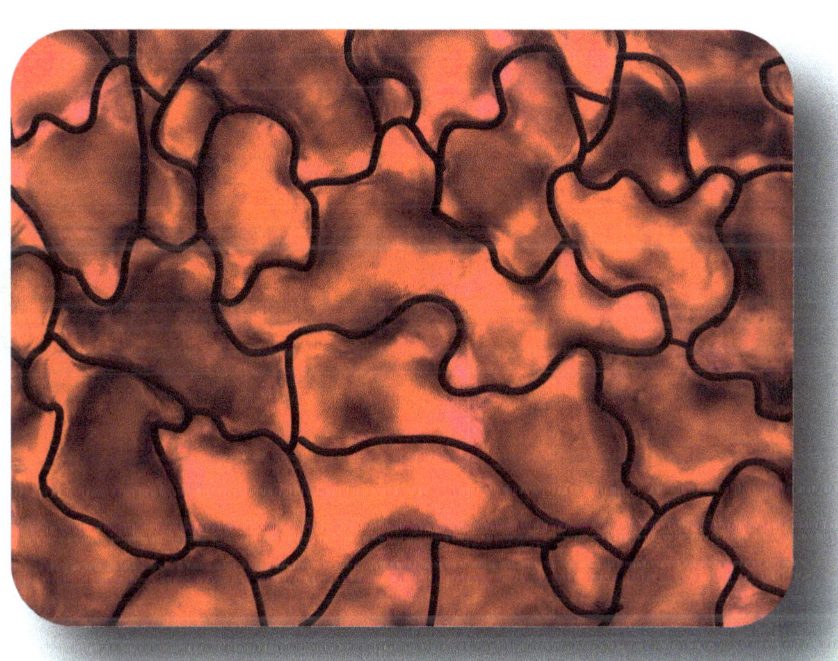

Cryptocoryne Wendtii (Green area)

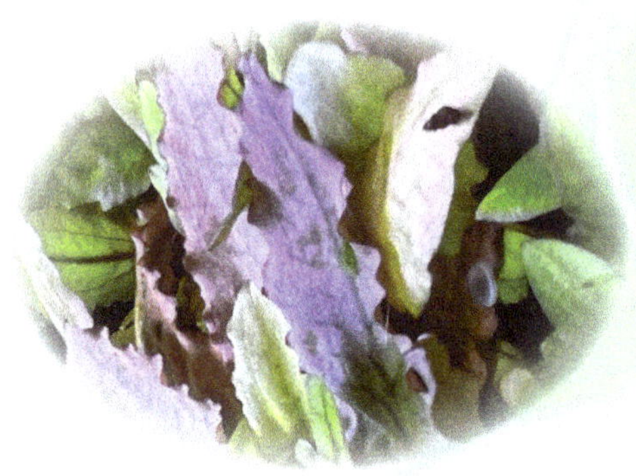

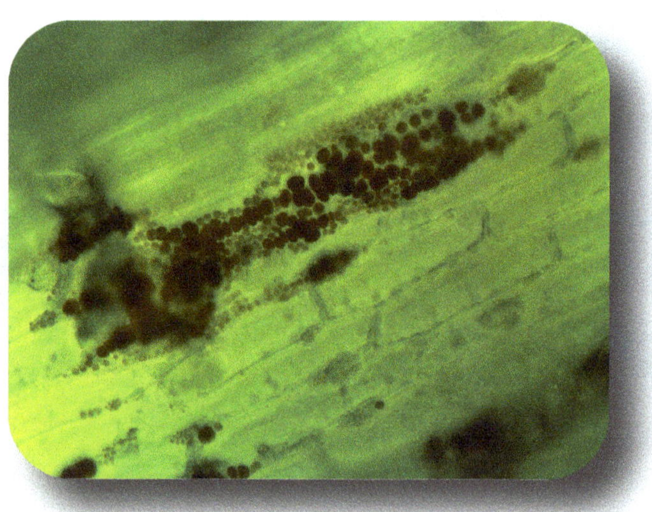

Aquarium Cryptocoryne Wendtii Leaf (green part), 200X, unstained, peeled. *This is an aquarium plant (green part) under a microscope. The square, tile-like things are cells, and the large area of black bubbles are parasitic organisms growing on the leaf due to its being an aquatic plant.*

When outlining and tracing, this can look like a drawing of a flying reindeer coming to deliver presents underneath the tree on Christmas Eve!

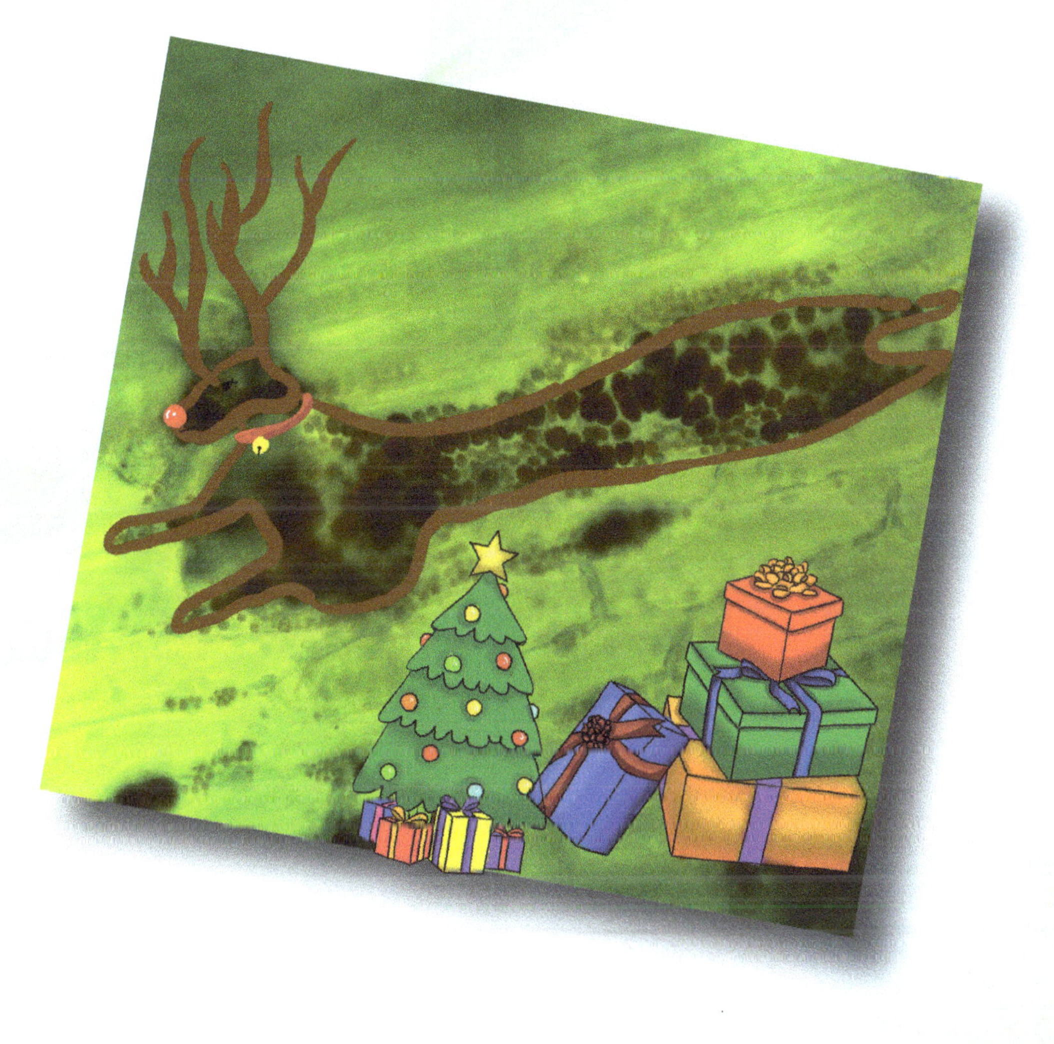

Cryptocoryne Wendtii (Red area)

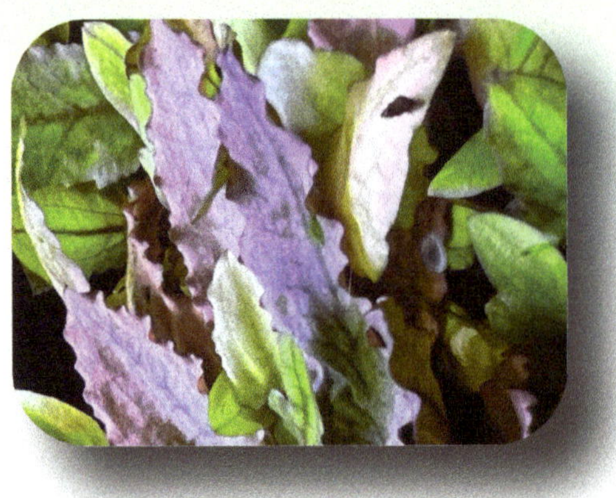

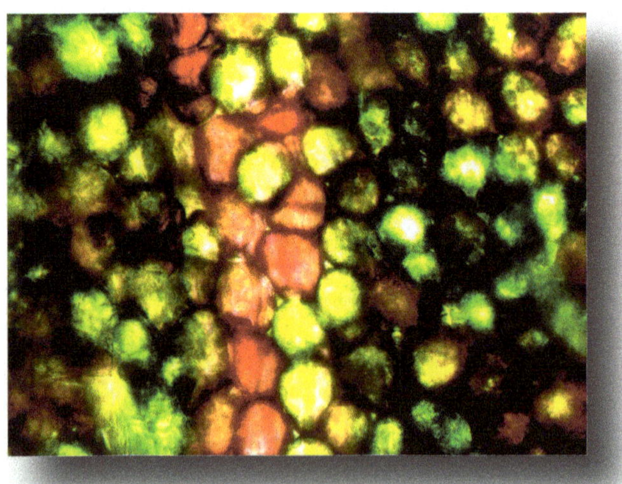

Cryptocoryne Wendtii Leaf, 200x, unstained, cross section. *The main notable details include the red, orange, yellow, and green cells that are bunched together tightly. These cells are responsible for the unique coloring of the plant.*

If you add the image into a bowl, it can look like a bowl full of crunchy, sweet cereal. Don't forget the milk! There is also a moist muffin on the side to complement the delicious cereal, which is a convenient and yummy breakfast that many people enjoy.

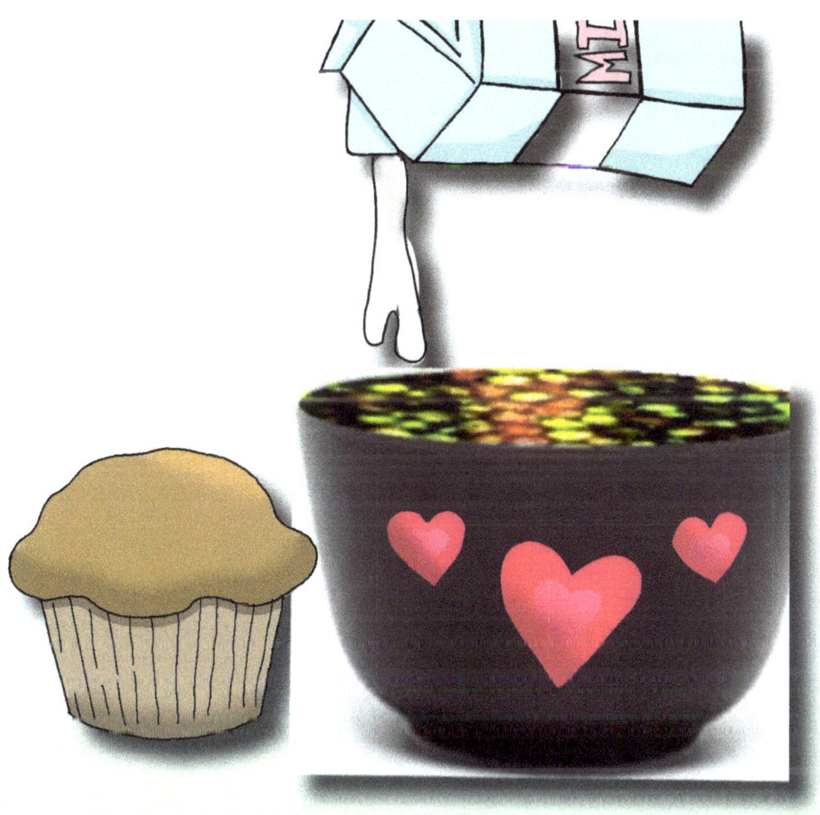

Fern Leaf

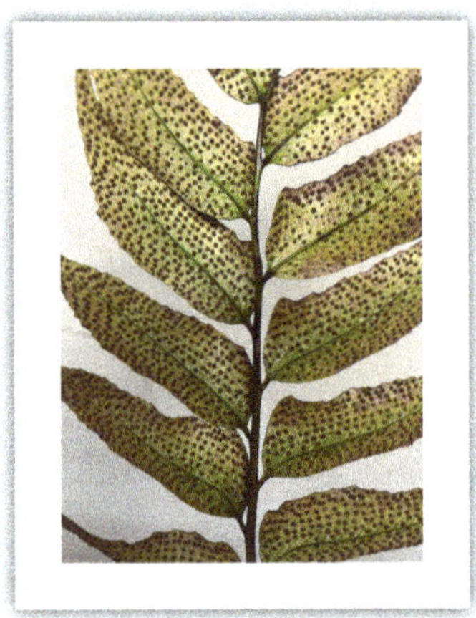

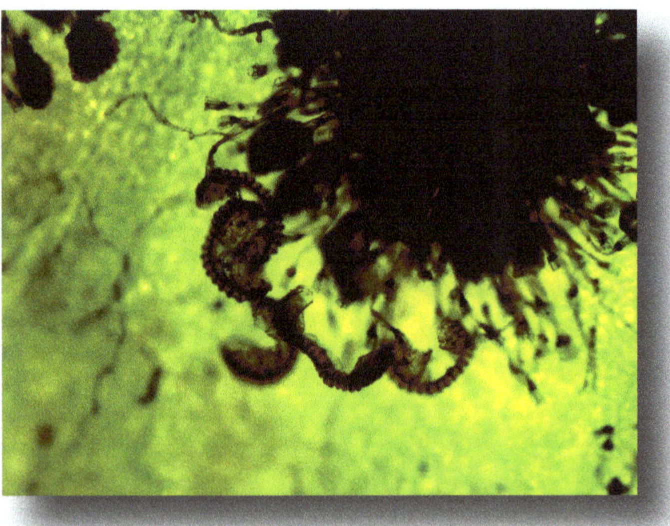

Fern Leaf, 40X, unstained, uncut. *The brown/black shape in the corner is a sporangium. Inside the sporangia are spore-producing cells called sporogonial cells.*

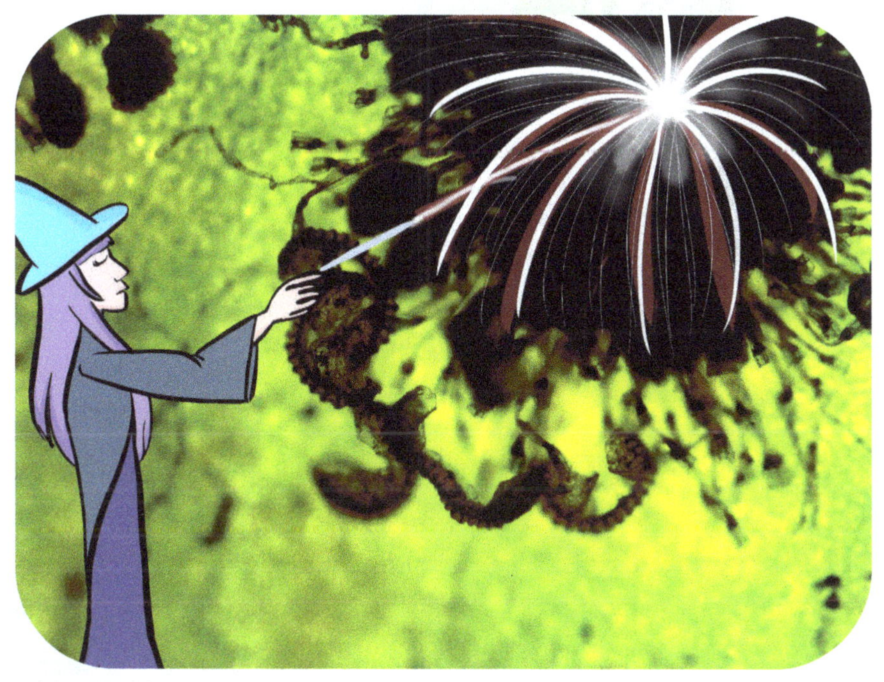

A wizard is chanting. Suddenly, a bright jet of light shoots out of her wand like a shooting star and blasts into a firework. Wizards are a popular aspect of fantasy adventures and folklore. She is using her magic to create explosions for sowing the seeds.

Gardenia Thunbergia Pistil

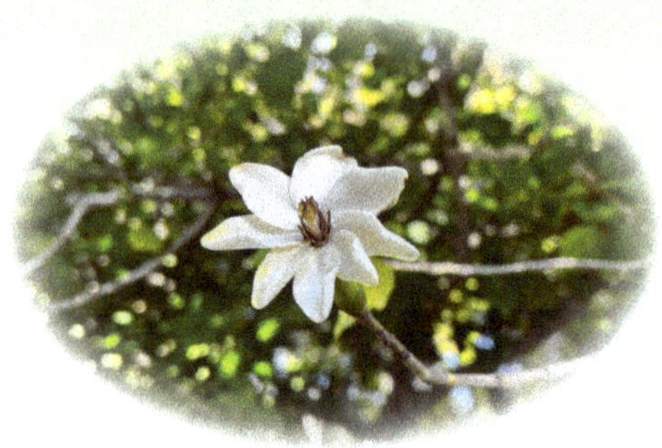

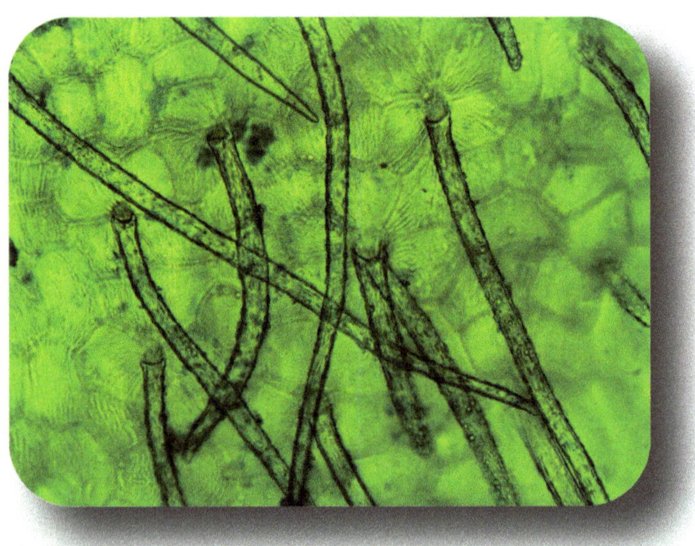

Gardenia Flower Pistil, 200X, unstained, cross section. There are long, thin, tube-like projections on the surface. The light hexagonal shapes in the background are cells. Some of the cells (if you look really closely) are textured a lot like fingerprints.

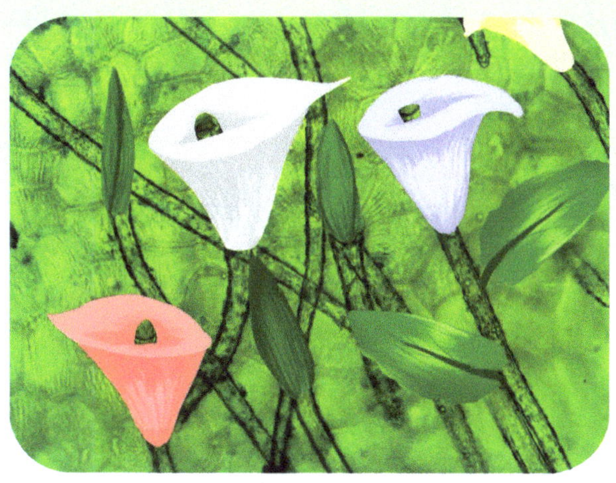

After adding bell-shaped petals and leaves, we can transform the flower Gardenia into Calla lilies. Calla lilies are the subject of many paintings, they also help embellish households with their vibrant shapes and colors.

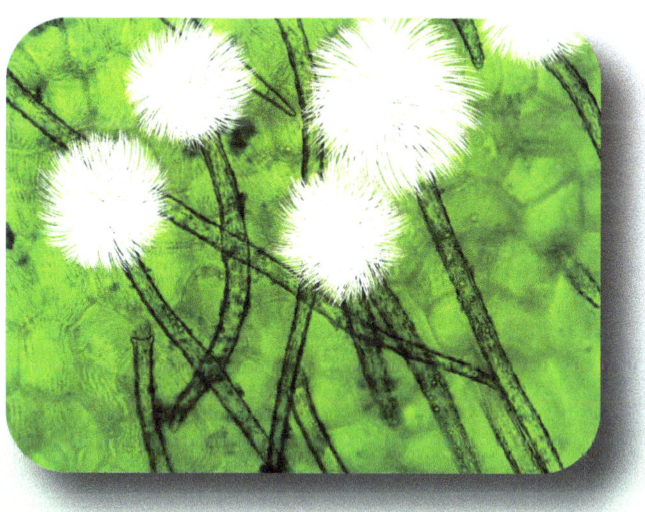

When you add fluff, it looks like the dandelion plant as it bil lows in the wind. The background is a grassy meadow.

Gingko Leaf

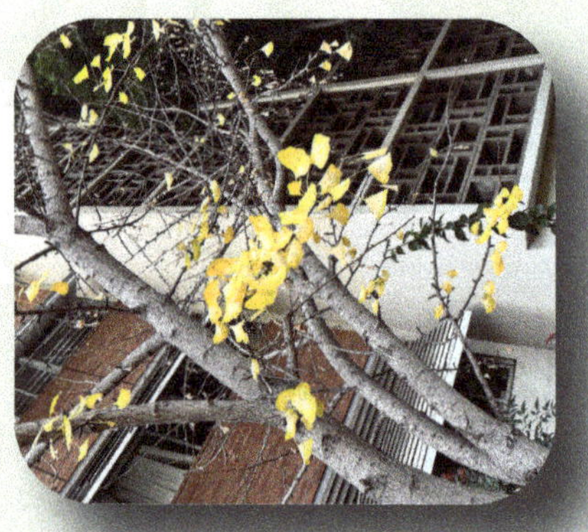

This is a gingko tree planted on the UCLA campus in honor of Professor T.H. Lin for his 90th birthday and his valued contributions to the university. He was incredibly hard-working, retiring when he was 102 years old.

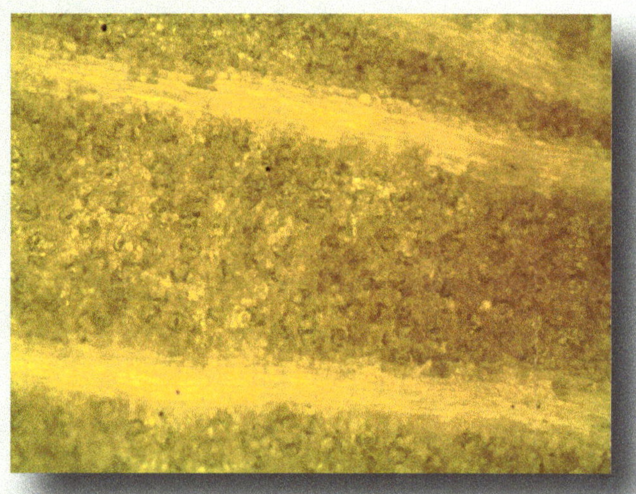

Gingko Leaf, 40x, unstained, longitudinal section. Gingko leaves are well known for their beautiful and vibrant yellow colors, which appear during autumn. The little 'squiggles' are the cells along the leaf stem, which transport nutrients and water to the leaves.

If you make a few simple adjustments, it can look like a road with
two children safely playing tag on a
sidewalk beside it.

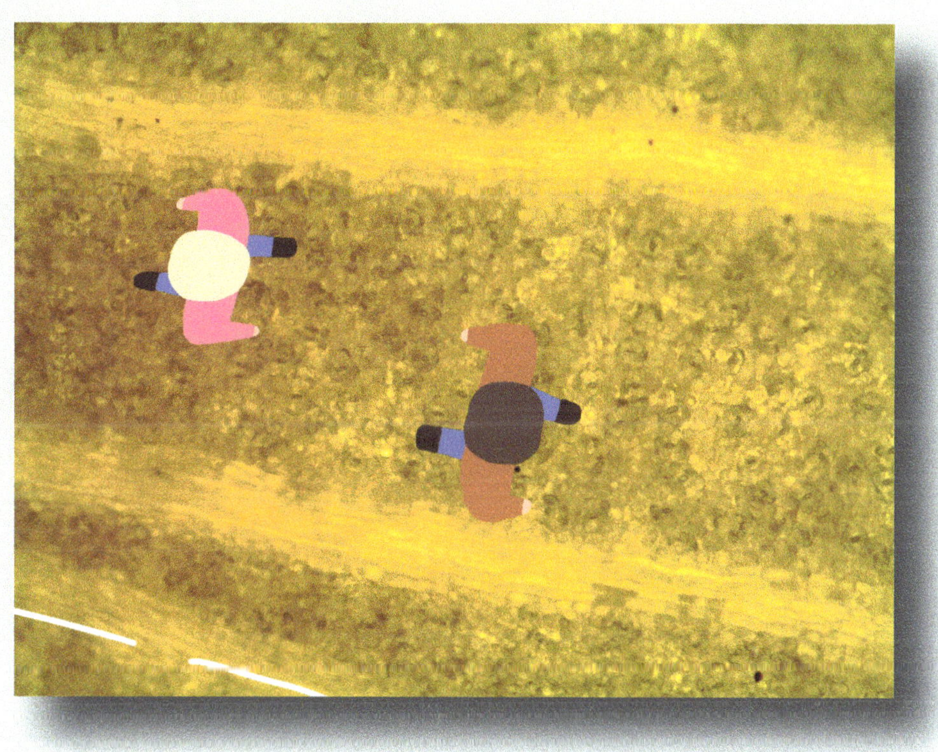

Heavenly Bamboo Leaf

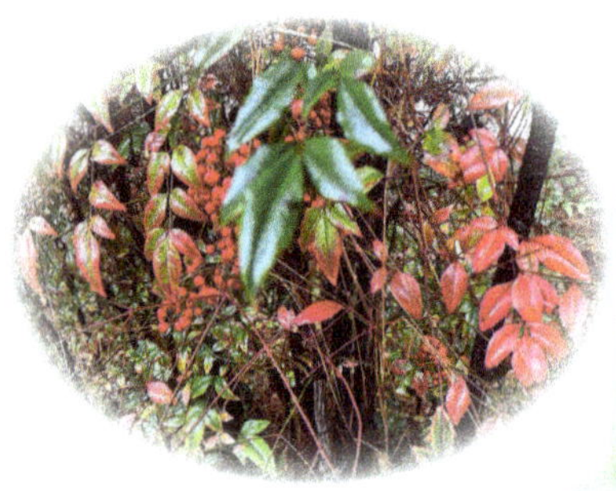

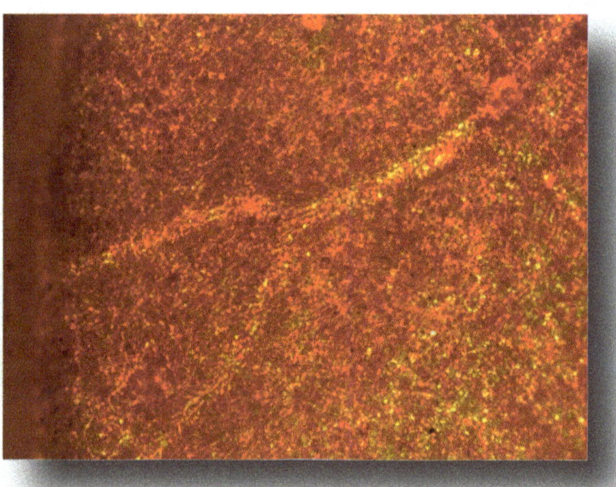

Heavenly Bamboo Leaf, 40x, unstained, peeled. The Heavenly Bamboo leaf is made of cells, which are the many red and yellow dots you see here. The leaf becomes red and yellow because the cells lose their green coloration (chlorophyll) in the autumn. If it wasn't autumn, it would be a lively green. The lighter colored pathways are the veins that transport important nutrients through the leaf.

This picture shows a little quiet home on a mountain next to a river. The stones on it are a makeshift bridge to get to the other side. It is autumn, and everything has taken a reddish hue. Soon it will be winter, then spring, when the plants will flourish again.

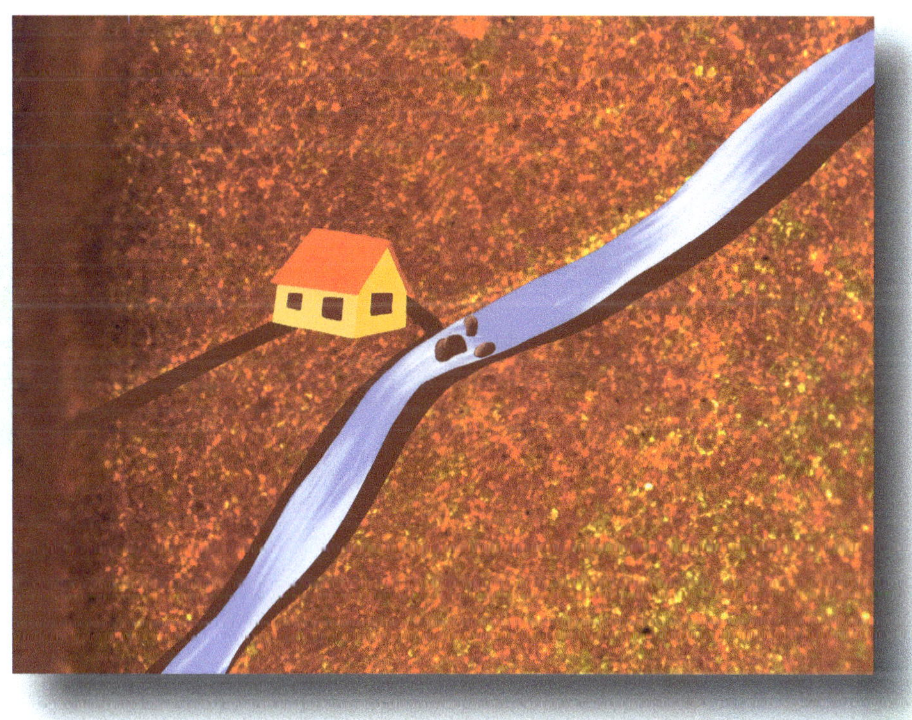

Rosemary Leaf

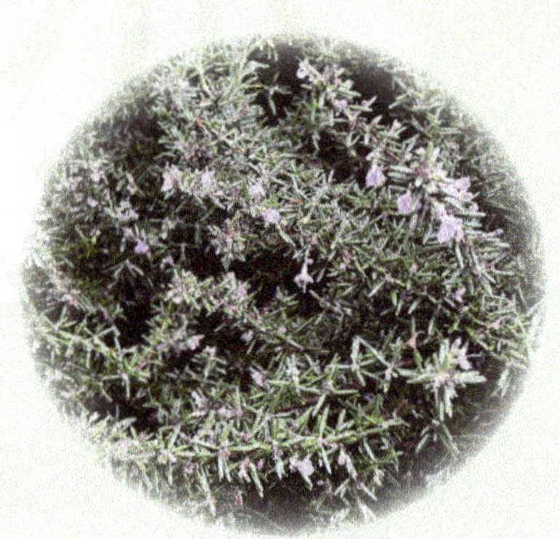

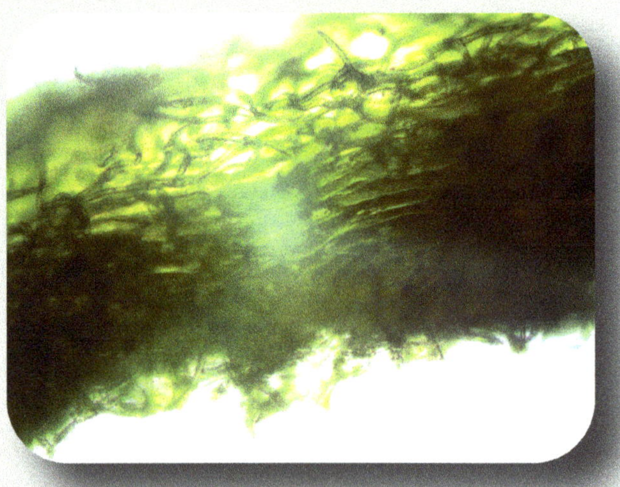

Rosemary Leaf, 200x, unstained, longitudinal sectioning. Rosemary resembles a thick, textured vine. The hair-like things are trichomes, which are oil-secreting organs that produce a wide range of substances and are there to protect the plant and repel bacteria and other things that could cause the plant harm.

This is a rosemary leaf underneath a microscope. It reminds us of a tree branch, so we added a basket filled with smooth large eggs—and now it is a bird nest!

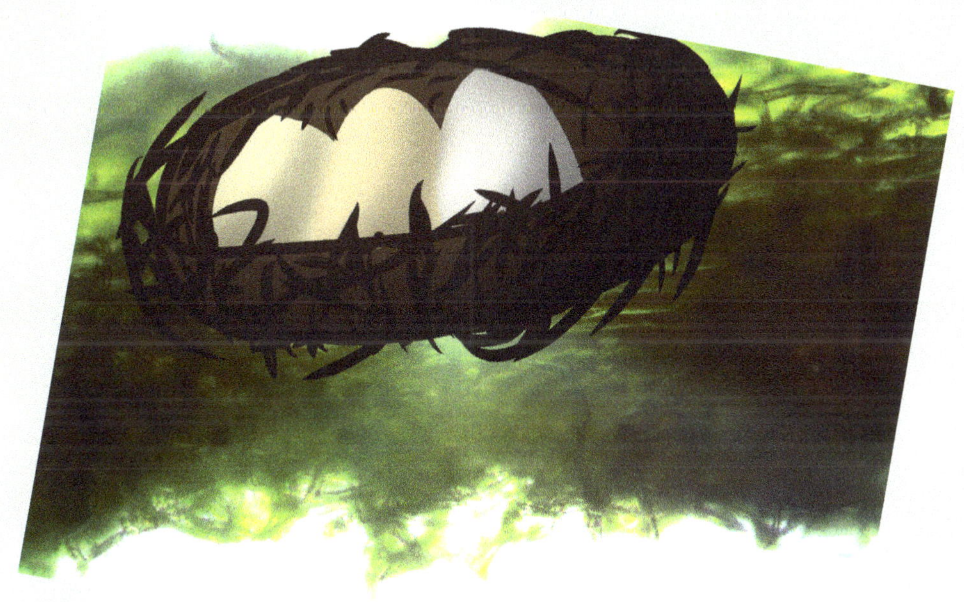

Strawberry Tree Flower

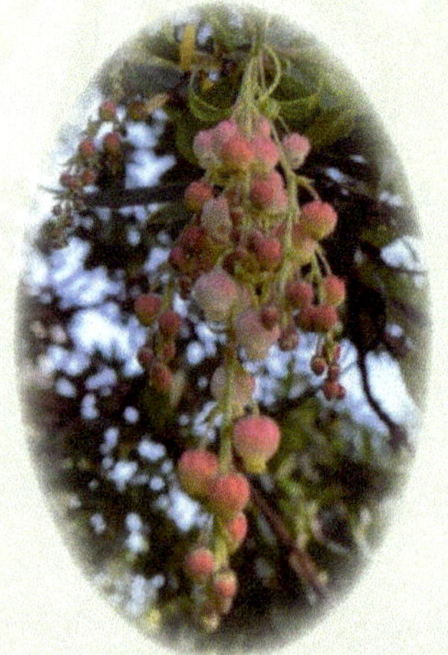

Strawberry tree flowers are pink, light green at the tips, and bell shaped. It is colloquially called strawberry tree because its bright red fruits somewhat resemble strawberries.

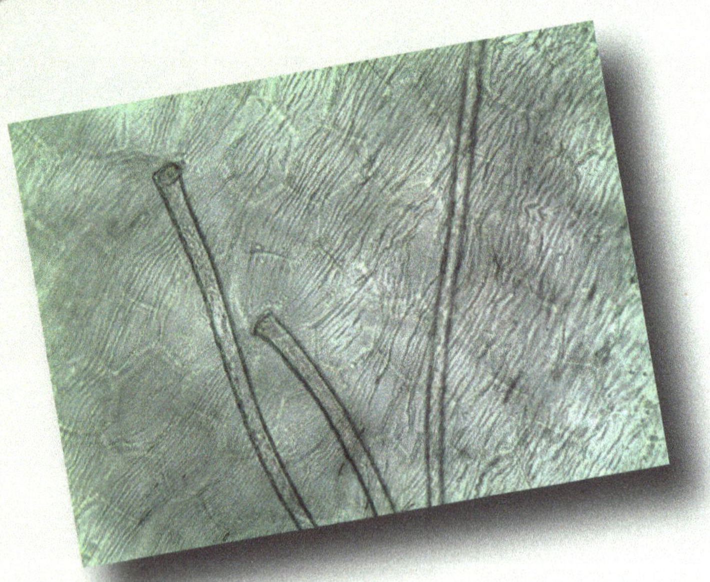

Strawberry tree flower, 200X, unstained. The long strands are the hairy structures that help pollination of the flowers. The lightly colored hexagon shapes in the back are the cells that make up the inner wall of the bell-shaped flower.

If you imagine that the hairy structures look like stems, with a simple modification, this can be transformed into a patch of lovely Dandelions. Dandelions have the lightest seeds and can travel around 3-4 miles! It is a pleasure to pick up a dandelion and blow on it to watch the seeds get scattered to grow new ones. It is truly a sight!

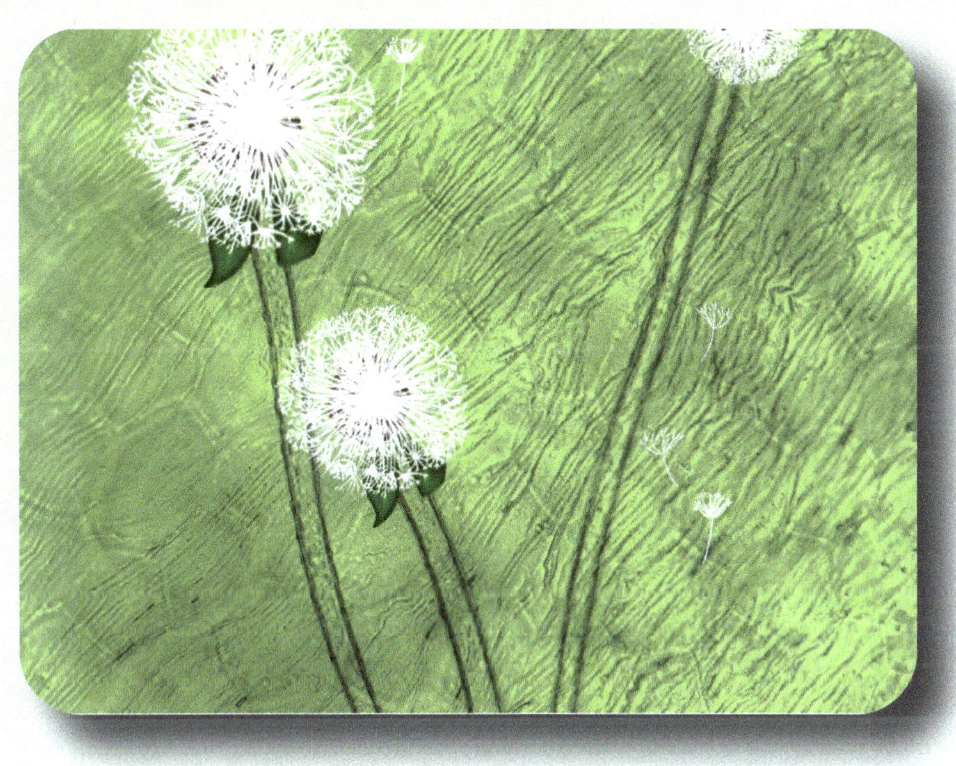

Succulent Leaf

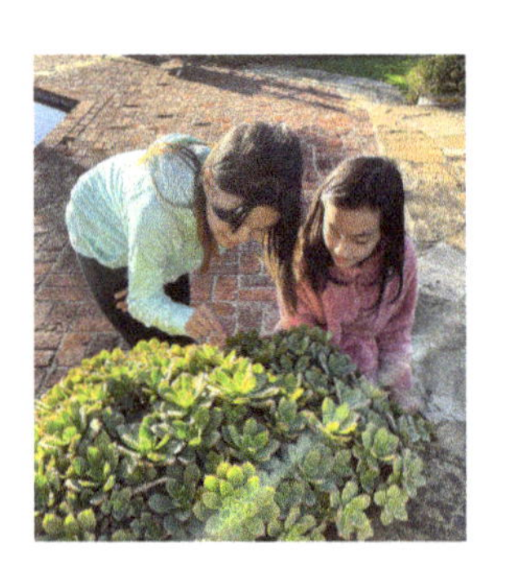

Succulent leaves store water and are so beautiful under sunshine!

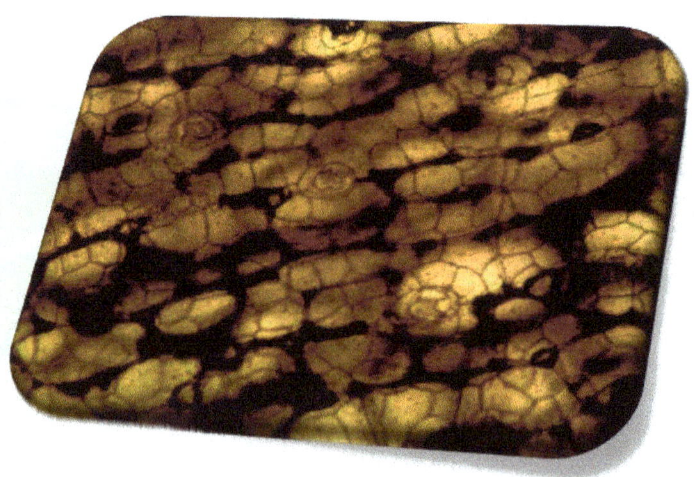

Succulent Leaf, 100x, iodine stained, cross section. There are more cells around the stomates (also called stomas) due to the way the plant cells are structured. Succulent cells have very flexible shape. Stomates are the breathing holes for the plant to attain nutrients such as air.

When enhancing and coloring in the lines, this can look like a blooming bush full of fresh colorful roses that are fragrant and majestic in the spring, summer, and autumn seasons.

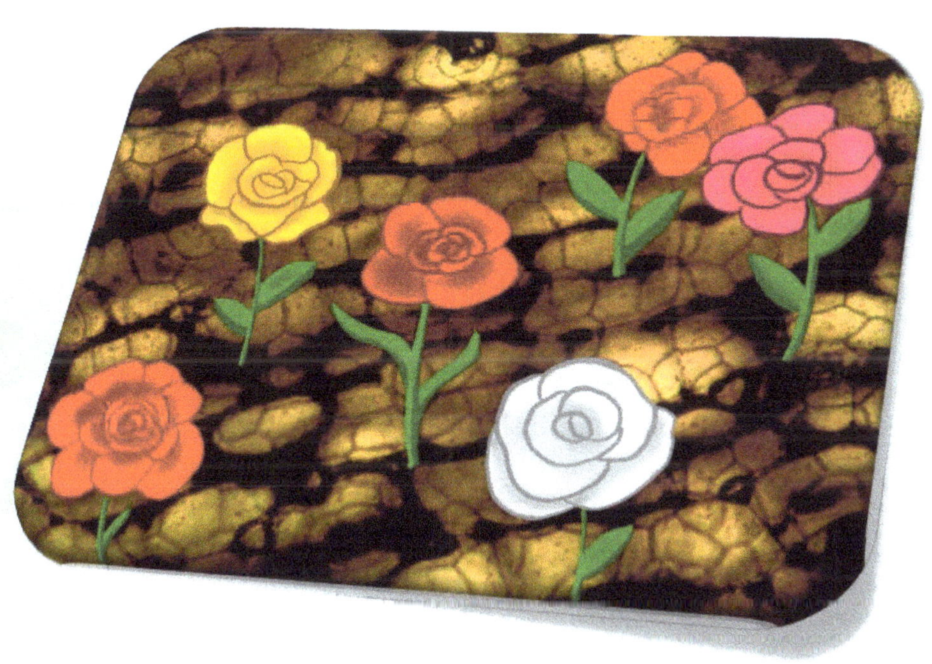

Yellow Jacobinia Stamen

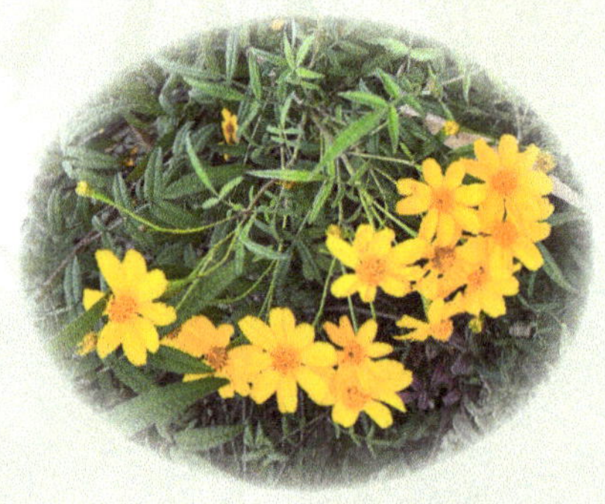

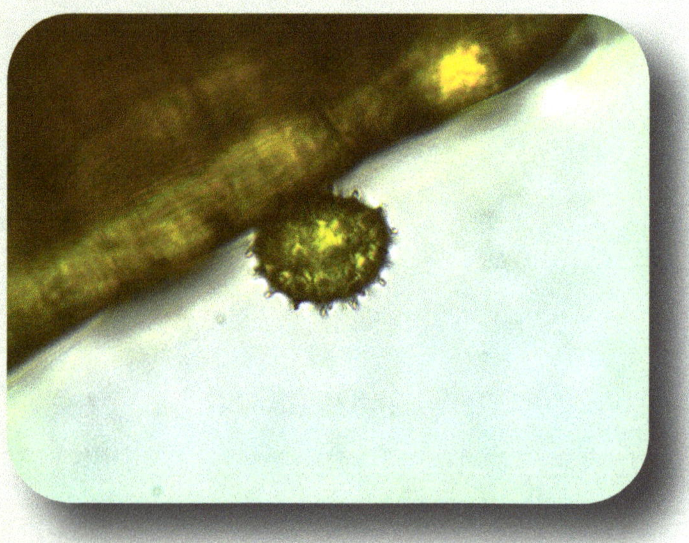

Yellow Jacobinia Stamen, 400x, unstained, uncut. This is a single pollen grain (particle of pollen) stuck to the side of the stamen of a yellow flower. The pollen can stick because of the tiny spikes on the surface, which are also used to latch on to insects when they come to pollinate.

With a few simple changes, the pollen now looks like an ant hanging off the branch of a tree. The ant is crawling towards a trail of crumbs. Where is it coming from?

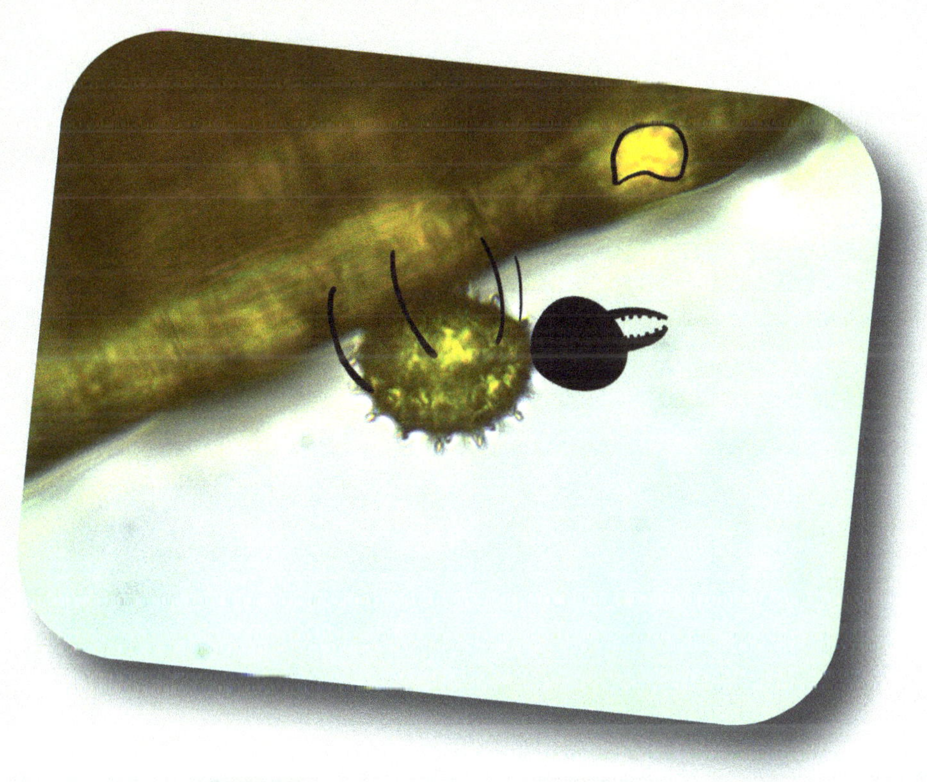

More to Explore

The diversity of pollen under the microscope may inspire budding scientists to recognize that there is more to the world than what the naked eyes typically see. This offers opportunities to see something new and to feel the fun of discovery.

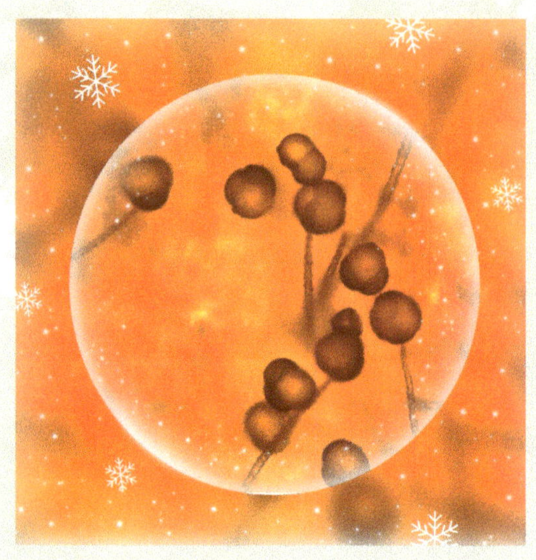

Bayberry tree flower pollen, 200x

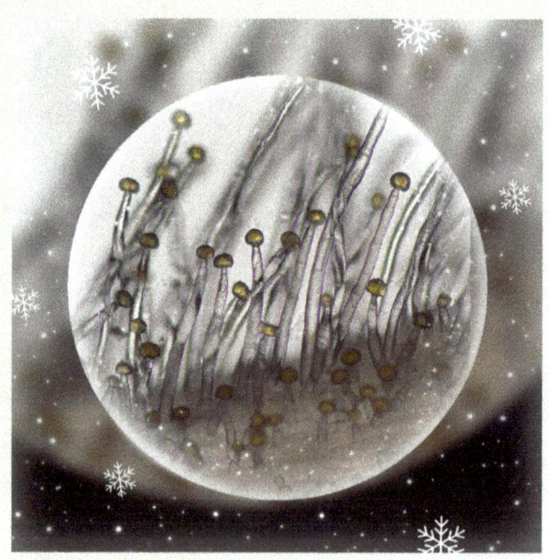

Jacaranda flower pollen, 100x

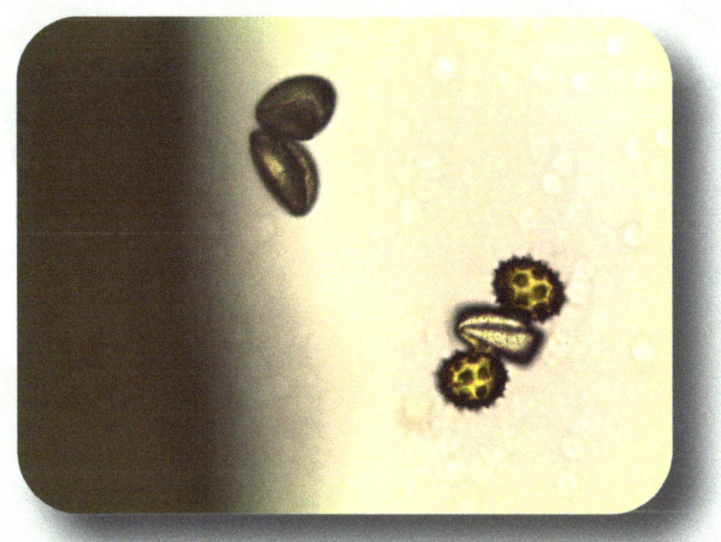

Golden trumpet tree flower pollen, 200x

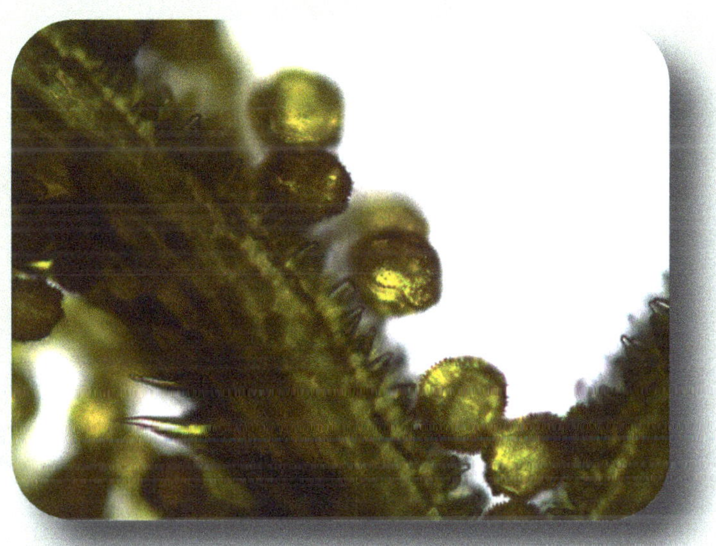

Dandelion flower pollen, 200x

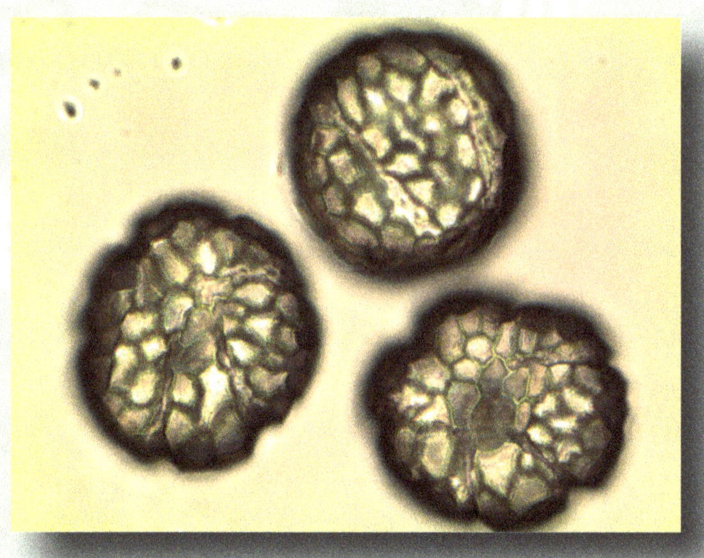

Basil flower pollen, 400x

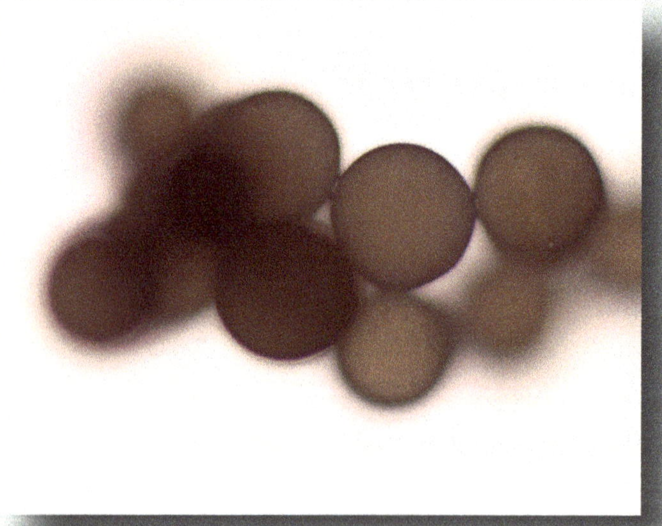

Canna lily pollen, 200x

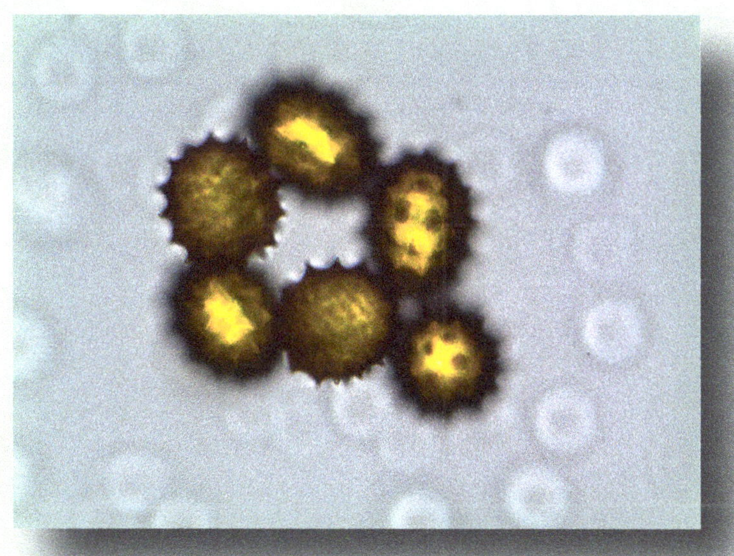

Cape marguerite pollen, 400x

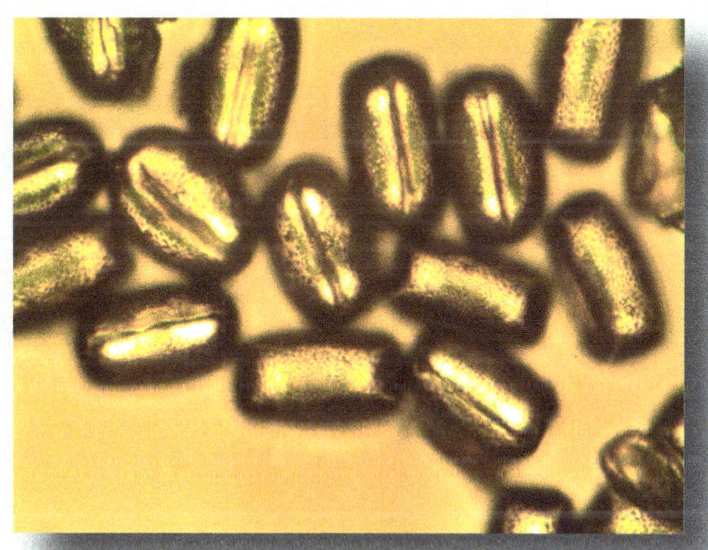

Chinese wisteria pollen, 400x

Dandelions are incredibly beautiful plants that have the lightest seeds. People have lots of fun blowing them off their stem and watching them bloom everywhere. And funnily enough, before that, they are beautiful yellow flowers as bright as the sun.

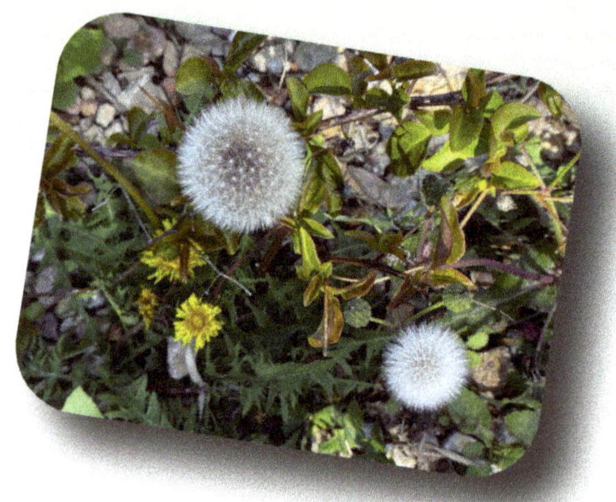

Different parts of a dandelion look so beautiful under the microscope, so here are a few for your enjoyment.

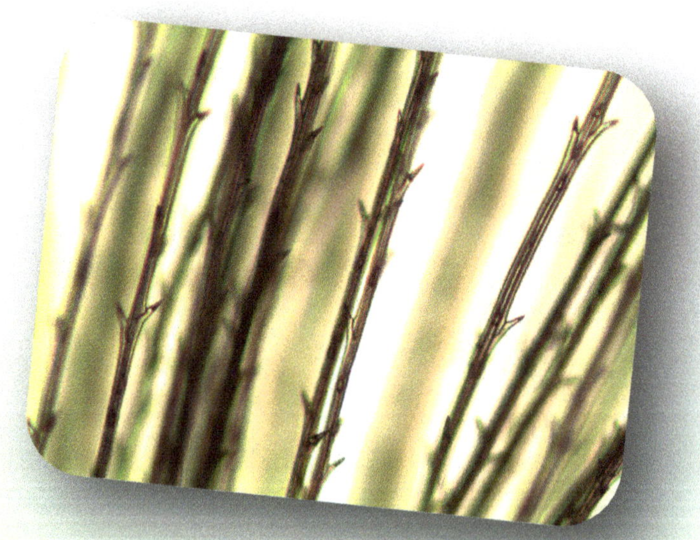

Dandelion fluff, 100x, unstained, uncut

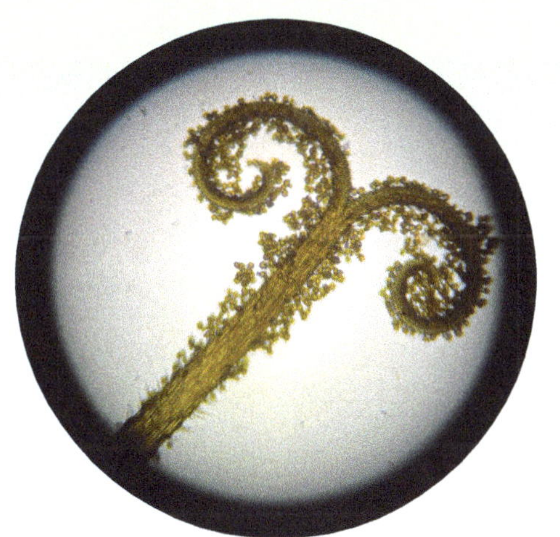

Dandelion flower sta-
men with pollen, 40x, un-
stained, uncut

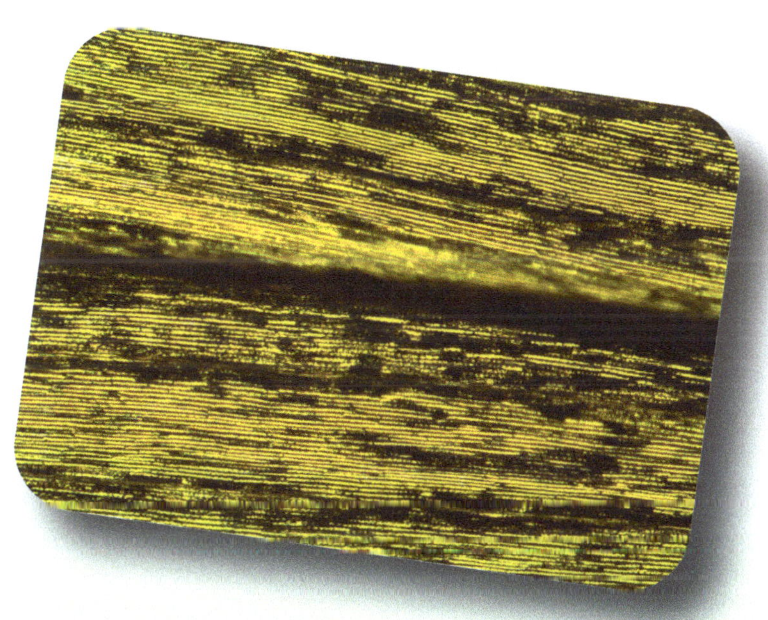

Dandelion flower petal, 40x, unstained, uncut